Cambridge English

Compact
First for Schools

Second Edition

Workbook with answers

Barbara Thomas
Laura Matthews

Cambridge University Press
www.cambridge.org/elt

Cambridge English Language Assessment
www.cambridgeenglish.org

Information on this title: www.cambridge.org/9781107415720

First published 2013
Second edition 2014

Printed in Dubai by Oriental Press

A catalogue record for this publication is available from the British Library

ISBN 978-1-107-41556-0 Student's Book without answers with CD-ROM
ISBN 978-1-107-41560-7 Student's Book with answers with CD-ROM
ISBN 978-1-107-41567-6 Teacher's Book
ISBN 978-1-107-41577-5 Workbook without answers with Audio
ISBN 978-1-107-41572-0 Workbook with answers with Audio
ISBN 978-1-107-41558-4 Student's Pack (Student's Book without answers with CD-ROM and
Workbook without answers with Audio)
ISBN 978-1-107-41574-4 Class Audio CD
ISBN 978-1-107-41604-8 Presentation Plus DVD-ROM

Additional resources for this publication at www.cambridge.org/compactfirstforschools2

The publishers have no responsibility for the persistence or accuracy of URLs
for external or third-party internet websites referred to in this publication, and
do not guarantee that any content on such websites is, or will remain, accurate
or appropriate. Information regarding prices, travel timetables, and other factual
information given in this work is correct at the time of first printing but the
publishers do not guarantee the accuracy of such information thereafter.

CONTENTS

1 FAMILY AND FRIENDS

Listening Part 3

Think about your best friend. Look at A–H in the Exam task below and decide which are important for you. Mark them in order of importance.

Exam task

🎧 **02** You will hear five short extracts in which people are talking about their best friend. For questions **1–5**, choose from the list (**A–H**) what each speaker particularly likes about their friend. Use the letters only once. There are three extra letters which you do not need to use. Play the recording twice.

A My friend has the same sense of humour as me.

B My friend shares the same memories as me.

C My friend has given up arguing with me.

D My friend always supports me.

E My friend has the same tastes as me.

F My friend tolerates my mistakes.

G My friend has the same career aims as me.

H My friend understands my feelings.

Speaker 1		1
Speaker 2		2
Speaker 3		3
Speaker 4		4
Speaker 5		5

Grammar

Prepositions and determiners with days and times

1 👁 Complete the sentences with *all, at, every, in, on* or nothing (-).

1 We'll be able to spend time together .... the evenings.

2 The programme will be shown on TV .... the summer.

3 My friends and I go shopping .... weekend.

4 I went to the school library .... lunchtime today.

5 I usually get home at four o'clock .... the afternoon.

6 I go swimming .... Wednesdays.

7 I'm going to play football .... next Saturday.

8 I usually visit my grandma .... the afternoon on Sundays.

9 On Saturdays I spend .... afternoon with my friends.

10 The bells always ring .... exactly midday.

Comparisons

2 👁 Complete these sentences with one word.

1 My older brother is much thinner .... my younger brother.

2 My mother is a .... deal older than my aunt.

3 I'm not .... good at maths as my cousin is.

4 My parents were always happier .... stay at home in the summer than go away.

5 I get .... more pocket money than my little brother.

6 The rivers dry up in summer because there is far .... rain than in winter.

7 Jane is .... good at playing the piano as I am, although she hasn't been learning for long.

8 The louder my brother shouted, the .... angry my granny got.

9 The more I play tennis, ... better I become.

10 The more homework I get, the .... time I have to see my friends.

Reading and Use of English Part 5

Exam tip ⟩

In Reading and Use of English Part 5, there are always six multiple-choice questions about one text. The text below is shorter than in the exam and there are only three questions.

1 Read the text below quickly and answer these questions.

1 Who are the two people?
2 What are they looking at?
3 Why is the writer surprised?

I was out shopping with my older sister. We were looking in the window of a tiny shop where there was an amazing display celebrating the festival which takes
line 4 place every four years in the city. It was better than anything we'd ever seen, especially in a shop like this. Although it's in the main shopping street and really popular with certain kinds of people, it sells really boring kitchen equipment and would never normally attract our attention. The centrepiece was a cake made to look like the town hall. Around the edge were little cup cakes, each with a figure from history made of sugar on top of it. While we were standing there, my sister suddenly said, 'I helped make some of those cup cakes.'
'But you can't even fry an egg,' I replied.
'I did it at school in cookery.'
'But you never said anything.'
'Well, I wanted to give everyone a surprise. Anyway, you wouldn't have believed me.' She turned away from
line 20 me. I called after her, 'I still think you're having me on. You want me to tell everyone and then you'll all have a good laugh.'
'Up to you.' And she was gone.

2 Look at the questions below, and before you decide on your answer to each question, read the tip before it.

Most Reading and Use of English Part 5 tasks have a question which asks you what a word or phrase refers to.

1 Look at the question below. Find 'it' and the words in the options in the text and underline them. Now read the sentences containing the words you have underlined.
What does 'it' in line 4 refer to?
A the city
B the festival
C the display
D the shop

Sometimes a question refers to ideas rather than actual words in the text.

2 Find 'a shop like this' in the text and underline it. All the ideas below are mentioned in the text but which one is referred to by 'like this'? Read before and after 'like this'.
When the writer says 'a shop like this', he is referring to the fact that
A he hadn't realised why the shop was usually so popular.
B the shop is not one he would normally take any notice of.
C he wishes the shop sold something he was interested in.
D the shop is in an important area for shopping in the city.

Most Reading and Use of English Part 5 tasks have a question which asks you about the meaning of a word or phrase. You will need to find its meaning by reading that section of the text carefully.

3 Underline 'you're having me on' in line 20 and read the whole conversation to decide what the writer means. Underline the words which help you.
What is meant by 'you're having me on' in line 20?
A You're teasing me.
B You're confusing me.
C You're criticising me.
D You're annoying me.

Vocabulary

Words often confused

1 **Complete the sentences with the correct word or expression. Use a dictionary if you need to.**

1 Some verbs and nouns go together to give a particular meaning. Complete each sentence with the correct word from the box.

involve make play produce

A Replacing some of the football team didn't .... the result the teacher wanted.

B Taking the main role in the school play would .... a lot of rehearsals.

C Computers .... a part in almost everything we do nowadays.

D Museums should .... an effort to interest young people.

2 Some words might not fit in the gap grammatically. For example, only one of these verbs can be followed by an adjective. Complete each sentence with the correct word from the box.

change get happen increase

A Riding a bicycle to school every day can .... tiring.

B If the pool is rebuilt, its prices will .... to almost double what they are now.

C You can .... your lifestyle and be more healthy.

D The bus was full yesterday – I hope it doesn't .... again today.

3 These words are all used to talk about how large something is. Sometimes the answer may depend on both grammar and meaning. Complete each sentence with the correct word from the box.

amount number size total

A I had a .... of five euros left after we'd bought everything we needed.

B The .... of energy we use every day is increasing.

C The .... of the horse you'll ride depends on your height and weight.

D A small .... of children are educated at home.

4 Sometimes you have to look at the position of the word in the sentence as well as its meaning, especially with adverbs. Complete each sentence with the correct word from the box.

deeply highly hugely particularly

A It is .... likely that school will be closed tomorrow because of the snow.

B Attendance at the concert was .... underestimated by the organisers and there wasn't enough room for everyone.

C I always sleep .... when I go camping.

D The children .... enjoyed the interactive displays.

Relationships

2 **Check the expressions in the box in a dictionary if you need to. Then complete each sentence with one of the expressions, putting the verb into a suitable tense.**

fall for   fall out with   get on well with get to know   go out together hit it off   socialise   take after

1 I met Jade when we started this school. We were both 11 and we .... straight away.

2 My brother, who .... our grandfather, has green eyes and red hair.

3 I .... most people because I'm easy-going and cheerful.

4 I .... Katie, who lives next door to us, last summer because she borrowed my bike without asking and we've never spoken to each other again.

5 My sister met her boyfriend at work and they .... now for three years.

6 Going to school helps young children learn to .... as well as teaching them to read and write.

7 I sit next to Claire in maths every day but we .... each other gradually because neither of us chats that much.

8 My mum and dad met at a party and .... each other there and then. They got married a few months later.

Exam task

For questions 1–8, read the text below and decide which answer (A, B, C or D) best fits each
gap. There is an example at the beginning (0).

Example:

0 **A** familiar   **B** sensitive   Ⓒ aware   **D** experienced

Twins

Unless you are a twin yourself, you are not
(0) .... of how it feels to have a sister or
brother born on the same day. Many twins even
have their own language when they are small.
(1) .... they usually grow out of this
secret communication, adult twins often know
what the other is thinking. This is particularly the
(2) .... with identical twins. Sometimes
if one twin gets hurt, the other one feels the pain
even if they know nothing about what is going
(3) ....

Some experts feel very **(4)** .... that twins
should be separated into different classes at school
so they develop as individuals, but this is not always
(5) .... to them. The best **(6)** ....
is usually to let the twins decide for themselves.
Sometimes because they look similar, twins play a joke
on other people, and change **(7)** .... with
each other. This idea, often used in films and plays,
(8) .... in some very funny scenes.

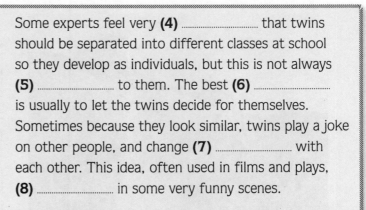

1 **A** So	**B** Although	**C** Because	**D** Despite
2 **A** fact	**B** condition	**C** event	**D** case
3 **A** on	**B** by	**C** ahead	**D** through
4 **A** highly	**B** greatly	**C** extremely	**D** strongly
5 **A** cooperative	**B** fortunate	**C** beneficial	**D** positive
6 **A** solution	**B** consequence	**C** explanation	**D** purpose
7 **A** locations	**B** places	**C** situations	**D** spaces
8 **A** develops	**B** produces	**C** results	**D** causes

Reading and Use of English Part 6

1 Read the text below about mountain climbing and answer these questions. Don't worry about the gaps in the text.

   1 Did the writer enjoy climbing mountains when he was small?

   2 Does he still enjoy it?

2 Read the text again and, for each numbered gap, choose A, B or C below.

My dad, mountains and me

My dad has always spent his free time climbing mountains. He spends ages planning his route, checking the weather forecast and finding the best maps, and he really likes a good challenge. **1** [   ] It means he feels he's really achieved something.

As soon as I could walk, he started taking me with him sometimes. At first, he used to carry me on his shoulders. **2** [   ] I can still remember how excited I was when we set off and how happy I felt.

The first time I did a proper climb with him I was about eight years old. As we came round the last bend to the summit, we saw some other climbers standing there admiring the view. They couldn't believe my father had managed to get to the top with such a small child. **3** [   ] When we were coming down, we met another family with two young girls, who must have been just behind us.

I'm now 15 and I belong to a local climbing club. Dad always hoped to pass on his love of climbing to me. **4** [   ] I already spend most of my weekends in the mountains. Sometimes Dad comes too but now I'm the one out in front and he can't always keep up with me!

1 **A** One possibility is that he always chooses the most difficult path up the mountain.
   B For example, he always chooses the most difficult path up the mountain.
   C By chance, he always chooses the most difficult path up the mountain.

2 **A** Since then, I had my own little boots and I followed him up the easiest slopes.
   B As a result, I had my own little boots and I followed him up the easiest slopes.
   C Later on, I had my own little boots and I followed him up the easiest slopes.

3 **A** In fact, we weren't the only ones who managed to do so that day.
   B In addition, we weren't the only ones who managed to do so that day.
   C Instead, we weren't the only ones who managed to do so that day.

4 **A** It seems that he will.
   B It seems that he would.
   C It seems that he has.

Listening Part 1

Exam task

🎧 **03** You will hear people talking in eight different situations. For questions 1–8, choose the best answer (**A, B** or **C**). Play the recording twice.

1 You hear a teacher talking to her class about a camping trip.
What does she say about weather conditions during the trip?
A Temperatures will be low at night.
B Heavy rain is expected on one day.
C Storms are possible at any time.

2 You hear two friends talking about a concert. The boy was surprised about
A the design of the concert hall.
B the way the lead violinist played.
C the range of music he heard.

3 You hear a girl talking to her brother.
Why did the girl go and see her teacher?
A to collect some notes
B to hand in some work
C to ask for advice

4 You will hear two friends discussing a rugby match they watched.
What happened during the match?
A A player was injured.
B A fan ran on to the pitch.
C The referee gave someone a warning.

5 You hear a boy telling a girl about a lesson he has just had.
How does the boy feel about it?
A It was less challenging than he expected.
B He might have made a bad choice.
C He realises he will have to work hard.

6 You hear a news report about a cycle ride.
It says that
A too many people took part.
B the conditions weren't suitable.
C some people behaved badly.

7 You hear a girl leaving a message on an answerphone.
Who has changed an arrangement?
A her father
B her friend
C her teacher

8 You hear two friends talking about surfing.
What does the boy think the girl would like about it?
A going to different places
B learning a new skill
C competing against others

🎧 **03** Listen again and try to write down the exact words that gave you the answer to each question. You can pause the CD as often as you like.

Grammar

used to and would

1 Are these sentences correct? Write C if they are and correct them if they are wrong.

1 I don't play tennis any more, but I used to.
2 When we lived outside the city, I would get up at six every morning to catch the school bus.
3 We would live in the city centre, but we live in the country now.
4 Joanna used to walk at least five miles every day.
5 When I was little, I would sit on the steps outside my house and watch the sun go down.
6 John would be able to play the guitar well once, but he's forgotten everything now.
7 Your cousin used to work in the shop on Saturday, didn't he?
8 I wouldn't like ice cream when I was young because it was too cold.

for, since and ago

2 Complete the sentences with *for, since* or *ago*.

1 Samantha's lived in the same house .... the whole of her life.
2 It's been a long time .... I went to the cinema.
3 When I spoke to Anna, she said she had landed safely in Berlin a short time ....
4 I studied in England .... three years, but I've returned to Spain now.
5 It was two years .... that I learnt how to scuba dive.
6 .... I've been living in Chile with my family, I've learnt a lot of Spanish.
7 I haven't been to the circus .... I was a young child.
8 My mother's been working as a teacher .... the last ten years.

Vocabulary

-ing and -ed adjectives

1 Complete the crossword with *-ing* and *-ed* adjectives formed from the verbs below. (You can use some of them twice.) Use the clues to help you.

> astonish disappoint embarrass
> exhaust fascinate impress relax
> worry thrill

Across

4 My mum likes to spend ages in the bath because she says it's ....

5 We were really looking forward to going to the new museum but the displays were very..................... .

9 I went on the fastest ride in the theme park and it was as .... as it said on the publicity.

11 I was so .... when my dad started to dance.

13 We were .... to see our cousin at the door because he lives in New Zealand.

14 Looking after my little brother is .... because he wants to run up and down all the time.

Down

1 I am .... by how the solar system works.

2 I was so .... when the trip to the seaside was cancelled.

3 My grandad's stories about his travels when he was young are .... – I don't mind how often he tells them.

6 I was .... with the Playstation my parents gave me for my birthday – it was just what I wanted.

7 Our teacher was really .... by our project – she gave us top marks.

8 It's .... to think that a few years ago none of us knew each other and now we're best friends.

10 I felt .... and very comfortable sitting on the sofa listening to music.

12 William was .... about travelling to London on his own as he'd never done it before.

Word building

2 Use one of the suffixes in the box to make a noun from each of the words. You may need to make some changes before adding the suffix.

> -ism -ship -ness

1 criticise ....
2 champion ....
3 dark ....
4 fit ....
5 friend ....
6 happy ....
7 ill ....
8 journalist ....
9 lazy ....
10 member ....
11 relation ....
12 weak ....

3 Use one of the suffixes in the box to make one or more adjectives from each of the words.

> -able -ish -ful -less

1 care ....
2 child ....
3 fool ....
4 harm ....
5 predict ....
6 price ....
7 profit ....
8 self ....
9 style ....
10 use ....

4 For each gap below, decide if you need a noun or an adjective, then choose from the words you made in Exercises 2 and 3 on page 10.

1 The new series of *The Teenage Detective* is so .... , I've guessed the ending each time so far.
2 The only .... the students had of the hostel was that there weren't enough showers.
3 It was very .... of you to eat the last piece of cake when you knew I was looking forward to it.
4 I've been working hard all day so you can't accuse me of .... !
5 Our team won the .... easily because we have three outstanding players.
6 The torch I'd brought was .... It was so faint you couldn't see anything with it.
7 They discovered a painting in the old man's house which was .... because it was by a really famous artist.
8 I thought Nick was much younger than he is because his handwriting is so ....
9 Cycling to school is a good way of improving my .... levels.
10 I wanted to join the gym but the .... fee is too expensive.

Reading and Use of English Part 3

Exam task

For questions **1–10**, read the text below. Use the word given in capitals at the end of some of the lines to form a word that fits in the gap in **the same line**. There is an example at the beginning (**0**).

Example: 0 EXCITEMENT

Sky-diving

People travel all around the world to experience the (**0**) .... of sky-diving. It attracts large numbers of young people who want to feel a sense of   **EXCITE**
(**1**) .... as they float through the air like a bird. It also makes a major   **FREE**
contribution to (**2**) .... in places like New Zealand.   **TOURIST**
A kind of sky-diving (**3**) .... took place in China about 1,000 years ago when people jumped from rocks and cliffs with a   **ORIGINAL**
parachute attached to them. Today sky-divers jump from an aeroplane flying at a (**4**) ....   **HIGH**
of about 4,000 metres. Those sky-divers who are (**5**) .... and may be diving for   **EXPERIENCE**
the first time are attached to an instructor who has spent many hours training. It is his or her
(**6**) .... to make sure everything goes smoothly and that the parachute opens at the right   **RESPONSIBLE**
moment. There is no room for (**7**) .... when you jump out of a plane! It sounds quite   **CARE**
(**8**) .... to me but most people love it.   **FRIGHTEN**

3 THE ENTERTAINMENT INDUSTRY

 **A**
 **B**
 **C**
 **D**

Listening Part 4

1 Which picture shows:

  1 a clown   3 a trapeze artist

  2 a tightrope walker   4 an acrobat

2 You are going to listen to Jasmine, a student at circus school. Read the exam questions carefully. Which of these things do you think you will hear about? Mark the ideas below with a tick (✓) or a cross (✗).

  1 a description of a day at circus school ☐

  2 information about Jasmine's family ☐

  3 what kind of circus work Jasmine enjoys ☐

  4 what the circus performers look like ☐

  5 how circus scenery is designed ☐

  6 advice about getting circus work ☐

  7 injuries that circus performers suffer ☐

Exam task

🎧 **04** You will hear an interview with Jasmine Chang, who is studying at circus school. For questions **1–7**, choose the best answer (**A**, **B** or **C**). Play the recording twice.

1 In what way does Jasmine think circus school is similar to other schools?
  A It's possible to study history there.
  B It's open for the same number of hours.
  C It has a very full timetable.

2 Why did Jasmine decide to attend circus school?
  A Her family were all in the circus.
  B She realised she could be a performer.
  C She wanted to learn gymnastics.

3 What kind of circus work has Jasmine already done in public?
  A performing a trapeze act with a friend
  B entertaining with a group of clowns
  C teaching children circus skills

4 Jasmine thinks that all circus performers make acts look easy by
  A improving their flexibility.
  B doing a lot of practice.
  C building up their strength.

5 What work behind the scenes does Jasmine recommend?
  A sound and lighting
  B set design
  C costume and make-up

6 What is Jasmine's attitude to getting work in a circus?
  A Get some temporary work if you can.
  B Wait until a job with a major circus comes up.
  C Avoid work that you find stressful.

7 Jasmine compares circus performers with ballet dancers to show that
  A enjoying your job is important.
  B training is more important for some jobs.
  C safety is an issue for all types of performer.

Vocabulary

Music

For each gap make a new word from one in the box.

classic	compose	conduct	guitar	music
record	rehearse	tradition		

1 All the .... in the orchestra stood up and bowed at the end of the concert.

2 Who was the .... of this piece of music?

3 We need to find a bass .... for our band.

4 The band spent several days in a .... studio when they were making the new album.

5 This is the last .... before the concert so everyone needs to be there.

6 The .... music of Chile is played on pipes.

7 I prefer rock or jazz to .... music.

8 It is important for an orchestra to watch the .... , who will keep everyone in time.

Reading and Use of English Part 7

1 Match each of the questions (1–10) with one of the statements (A–L) written by teenagers who are TV actors. There are two extra statements which you don't need to use.

Which person says they

are uncomfortable with criticism?	1
are confident about the future?	2
don't regret a choice they made?	3
appreciate their present situation?	4
were given some bad advice by someone?	5
were criticised by someone?	6
made a difficult choice?	7
have changed their attitude?	8
are grateful to someone?	9
like being challenged?	10

A   I had a teacher at school who first got me into acting and I might never have tried if he hadn't been so enthusiastic.

B   The director told me I was being too dramatic and he was right.

C   I never choose a role that I know I will find easy.

D   I realise how lucky I am that I can spend my time doing something I love.

E   I know my acting is just going to get better and better.

F   I had to decide whether to finish my exams or take a part in the TV show and in the end, I took the part.

G   I was offered a small part in a children's series and my mum thought it wouldn't do well, so I took a part in an adult drama instead which isn't nearly as successful.

H   I wish I had taken the advice I was offered early in my career.

I   I knew as soon as I was offered a part in the TV show that I wouldn't stay at school and it turned out to be the right thing to do.

J   I find it difficult if someone doesn't like what I do when I think I've done my best.

K   I took a part in a TV show which wasn't nearly as successful as I thought it would be.

L   At first I thought acting was an easy life but I'm now aware of how hard you have to work.

2   Now read what two boys said about being TV actors. For questions 1–8, choose A or B.

Which person

didn't think he'd done as well as he could?	1
finally got the chance he wanted?	2
has really benefited professionally from working with someone?	3
hopes to do something different in the future?	4
was worried he wouldn't do well?	5
was successful the first time he tried to get an acting job?	6
has made social connections through his work?	7
is concerned about the future?	8

A   Kyle

I applied for loads of auditions to try for different parts in theatre and TV and eventually I got the opportunity. I really wanted to do my best and I was afraid I wouldn't be able to because I felt nervous. But as soon as I got in front of the director, I forgot everything else and I got a tiny part in a school drama. I'm enjoying it and have made good friends among the other actors in the play – we do things together when we're not working. But I know this isn't an easy business and as I get older I may not be offered parts.

B   Sam

I had always loved acting at school but I hadn't really thought of it being a job in the future. But one day our teacher told us a TV company was looking for children to be in a drama series about a school. So I turned up for my very first audition and, although I didn't feel I managed to show the director what I am capable of, I got a small part. I now have a much bigger part in the drama. I know how lucky I am and I've learnt such a lot from the actor who plays my mum and is so experienced, but I'm thinking of trying to get onto a comedy show as I love making people laugh.

Vocabulary

Entertainment

Fill in the missing words in the text. The first letter of each word is given, and the number of dashes shows the number of letters. Then find the words in the word search below.

This summer several favourite programmes return to our TV **(1)** s _ _ _ _ _ _ _ _ but there are also some brand-new shows. I've had a quick look at the guest list of a new **(2)** c _ _ _ _ show to see who will be interviewed, and there are some really well-known **(3)** c _ _ _ _ _ _ _ _ _ _ there from film, TV, music and also sport. The **(4)** p _ _ _ _ _ _ _ _ _ is Don Makie and it's on every Friday at 9.30. I'm not sure how serious the interviews will be as Makie is more well known for his jokes as a **(5)** c _ _ _ _ _ _ _ so this is a completely new **(6)** r _ _ _ _ for him. If you want to know more about the stars and planets, there's a **(7)** d _ _ _ _ _ _ _ _ _ _ _ series on Monday evenings at 8.00. And of course, on **(8)** C _ _ _ _ _ _ _ Five, *The Kids from Kurzon Street*, the **(9)** s _ _ _ _ opera set on a Los Angeles housing estate, continues three times a week. It seems to be just as popular after five years. The main **(10)** c _ _ _ _ _ _ _ _ _ _, Louis, has been played by Sam Stromboli since the beginning but Sam is getting into films now so Louis may also have to move on.

C	D	B	E	I	S	E	A	S	D	P	S
E	H	O	T	D	P	E	E	N	R	R	C
L	C	S	C	S	C	T	S	E	T	E	R
E	E	O	I	U	R	H	T	T	I	S	E
B	L	E	M	N	M	C	A	O	A	E	E
R	E	D	C	E	A	E	U	N	A	N	N
I	O	A	H	R	D	P	N	L	N	T	S
T	E	E	A	R	A	I	F	T	C	E	T
I	K	H	T	O	O	O	A	E	A	R	L
E	C	T	S	C	C	L	E	N	N	R	S
S	E	H	T	L	T	R	E	F	E	H	Y
E	N	A	A	O	R	N	A	N	E	Y	T

Grammar

Linking words and phrases

1 Choose the correct word in italics.

1 Our new flat is big and on a busy road *but / even though* our old one was small and quiet.
2 *Despite / However* not feeling well, Jake managed to finish the race and come third.
3 My grandparents had a good life *in spite of / while* their lack of money.
4 You are expected to be at school between 8.15 and 3.15. If, *however / even though*, you have to leave the building, you should report to the office.
5 The police continued searching the house *despite / but* being almost sure the thieves had got away.
6 I tried calling on my friend *although / despite* I knew he probably wouldn't be in.
7 *In spite of / Even though* the fact that he didn't speak much Spanish, my dad managed to ask for directions.
8 I saw some trainers I liked *even though / but* I couldn't decide which to get.

The passive

2 Put these sentences into the correct form of the passive.

1 The school will include admission to the exhibition in the price of the trip.
Admission to the exhibition .... in the price of the school trip.
2 Are they filming that new drama series in Madrid?
.... that new drama series .... in Madrid?
3 The students have done all their homework on time.
All homework .... on time.
4 The drama teacher didn't give Jane the main role in the school play this time.
Jane .... the main role in the school play this time.
5 They were rehearsing the play in a tiny room. The room where the play .... was tiny.
6 Everyone has made their costumes for the play. All the costumes for the play ....
7 They were playing my favourite song when I walked into the room.
When I walked into the room, my favourite song ....
8 Our teacher has given us instructions for the concert.
We .... instructions for the concert.

have something done

3 Complete each sentence with an appropriate form of *have* and the past participle of one of the verbs in the box.

> clean   correct   cut   steal   install   paint   take   test

1 Mum is .... her coat .... as it's rather dirty.
2 Susan .... her hair .... on Friday because she was going to a party.
3 My parents are .... the outside of the house .... next month.
4 I .... my bicycle .... yesterday so I'm walking everywhere now.
5 I'm going to .... my eyes .... because I think I need glasses.
6 I .... my homework .... as soon as I handed it in.
7 We should .... central heating .... in our house last winter because it got so cold.
8 I .... my photo .... so I could send off for a new passport.

Reading and Use of English Part 4

Exam task

For questions 1–6, complete the second sentence so that it has a similar meaning to the first sentence, using the word given. **Do not change the word given.** You must use between **two** and **five** words, including the word given. Here is an example (0).

Example:

0 I haven't got much money so I would prefer to take a packed lunch with me.
RATHER
I haven't got much money so I ..*would rather take*.. a packed lunch with me.

1 I couldn't fix my bike myself so someone at the bike shop did it.
HAD
I .... by someone at the bike shop because I couldn't do it myself.

2 The teacher said the trip would go ahead despite the heavy rain that we'd had all night.
ALTHOUGH
The teacher said the trip would go ahead .... heavily all night.

3 My mother met a friend who she last saw three years ago.
FOR
My mother met a friend who she .... three years.

4 I hadn't been told about the extra homework because I had been ill.
NOBODY
I had been ill so .... about the extra homework.

5 Basketball isn't as popular as all the other sports played in my school.
LEAST
Basketball .... all the sports played in my school.

6 My little brother found that movie frightening.
BY
My little brother .... that movie.

Reading and Use of English Part 5

1   Match the adjectives in the box with their dictionary meanings.

> astonished disappointed discouraged
> embarrassed jealous suspicious

1   not trusting someone or something
2   feeling ashamed or shy
3   unhappy because something was not as good as you hoped or expected
4   very surprised
5   having lost your confidence or enthusiasm for something
6   unhappy or angry because someone has something you want

2   Read the paragraph below. How did the boy feel when he knew he hadn't been chosen for the team? Choose one of the adjectives from Exercise 1.

We all crowded round the list on the notice-board to see who was going to be in the team on Saturday. The match was important as it was against our main competitors. I quickly scanned the names and mine wasn't there, not even as a reserve. It wasn't a surprise because I had only taken up hockey in the last couple of terms. However, I had been optimistic because I was actually just as good as some of the others who had been on the team for years. I felt really down about it for a bit. But what I didn't have was the experience of playing as a member of a team

line 13   – the others were so tuned into each other's strategies, they could predict what was going to happen next without thinking about it. Mr Gilbey knew what he was doing when it came to choosing the team – it was really important we won the match and maybe my turn would come soon. I had heard that he had consulted the hockey captain and some of the other players when he was choosing, which seemed like a good system, but getting into the team was a bit like being a politician. You had to show you were good so they noticed you and voted for you. And that's what I would do.

3   Read the text again. Look at the verb 'tuned into', read the words around it and answer this question.

What does 'tuned into' mean in line 13?
A   helpful to   C   sympathetic to
B   inspired by   D   familiar with

4   Find the part of the text where the boy talks about being a politician and answer the question below.

Why does the boy compare the hockey team to politics?
A   to demonstrate the idea that the method of choosing players was unusual
B   to emphasise the fact that you had to prove you deserved a place
C   to complain about how long it took to be accepted by the other players
D   to highlight the fact that some of the players had too much power

Vocabulary

Sport collocations

1   Match a word from A with one from B to form sport expressions. Use each word only once.

A	beat energy football ice play score tennis win

B	court the cup a goal levels pitch the record rink rugby

2   Now complete the sentences with expressions from Exercise 1. Change the verb forms if necessary.

1   A huge cheer went up as the two teams walked on to the ....
2   Rebecca Smith .... today by going incredibly fast in the 100 metres freestyle.
3   My brother loves .... and is now in the national team, which plays South Africa on Saturday.
4   Manchester City won the match by .... in extra time.
5   Your .... remain constant if you eat a good diet and avoid sugary foods.
6   Ice hockey is a sport played on a(n) ....
7   Ajax baseball club .... in the competition and became the champions.
8   The player hit the ball into the corner of the .... and won the match.

Listening Part 2

Label the picture of people playing ice hockey with the words in the box. Use a dictionary to help you if necessary.

| goalie | ice | net | puck | skates | stick |

1
2
3
4
5
6

Exam task

🎧 **05** You will hear a teenager called Sam Lloyd talking to his class about ice hockey. For questions 1–10, complete the sentences with a word or short phrase. Play the recording twice.

Sam finds the (1) .... of an ice hockey game appealing.

Sam says that goalies are very (2) .... compared to other players.

Sam says there has to be a (3) .... on your team to every move your opponents make.

Sam claims that ice hockey is extremely (4) ...., because you need to focus on it so much.

On his beginners' course, Sam was taught about basic (5) .... as well as balance.

The next thing Sam learnt was (6) .... skills at coaching sessions.

Sam says that you should buy skates, gloves and a (7) .... immediately, but you can borrow other kit for a while.

Coaches make sure that players in junior club games are of the same (8) .... and age.

Sam says that a good month to start playing ice hockey is (9) ....

Sam thinks that his (10) .... has increased since he started playing ice hockey.

Vocabulary

make and *do*

1 Complete these sentences with *make* or *do*, then put the nouns into the correct column.

The basic meaning of .... is to perform an activity or job.
The basic meaning of .... is to create or produce something, and it is often used in idioms.

| arrangements   your best   changes   a course |
| a decision   your duty   an effort   friends |
| a good impression   homework   housework |
| a mistake   a noise   research   sport |
| a success of   a suggestion |

make	do

2 ⊙ Complete the sentences with *make* or *do* and a noun from the table above.

1 You must .... the .... for yourself, I can't advise you on what to do.

2 The student .... a .... on her teacher because she worked hard.

3 On school days, I always .... my .... at the kitchen table.

4 I'm going to .... a .... about the best way for you to finish your project.

5 You've .... the same .... several times in your essay, so check carefully.

6 If you see someone commit a crime, you should .... your .... and call the police.

7 My sister's .... a great .... of her new job; she's just got a promotion.

8 You should always .... your .... if you want to succeed.

9 Have you .... the travel .... for our trip yet?

10 You need to .... a real .... if you want to succeed next time.

Grammar

it and there

1 ⊙ Complete the sentences with *it* or *there* and a form of the verb *to be*.

1 .... a great swimming pool in the centre of town.
2 I heard on the weather forecast that .... a storm later.
3 .... a good idea to finish your homework before you go out.
4 .... a test in science today?
5 How far .... to the sports centre from here?
6 .... any rain for months, so nothing is growing.
7 .... a chance to check my work before I hand it in?
8 .... difficult to get home by 6.00 tomorrow?
9 .... at all difficult to learn to sing.
10 .... a clothes shop here before, but it's closed down now.

Prepositions

2 ⊙ Choose the correct preposition.

1 This necklace was a present *from* / *of* my aunt, who died last year.
2 When children get bored, they start complaining *for* / *about* everything.
3 This trip was organised by Katie's father: six different places *of* / *in* France in six days.
4 I went with Marina *to* / *in* her house and waited there for my friend Pablo.
5 I'm not sure if food is included *to* / *in* the cost of the trip.
6 If you want to meet at another time, call me *on* / *at* my mobile.
7 A TV company chose my school to make a film because we are the most popular school *in* / *of* Milan!
8 During the holiday, we'll go to a museum and *to* / *on* several excursions.
9 We can meet *at* / *to* my house.
10 The programme will be shown next Saturday night *at* / *on* Channel 3.

Modal verbs, *need* and *be able to*

3 Complete the second sentence so that it has a similar meaning to the first sentence, using the word given. Use no more than five words, including the word given.

1 It's important that I take my tennis racket tomorrow or I won't be able to play in the tournament.
REMEMBER
I .... take my tennis racket tomorrow or I won't be able to play in the tournament.

2 It's not necessary to buy a ticket in advance for the school concert.
NEED
You .... to buy a ticket in advance for the school concert.

3 It hasn't been possible for us to watch TV since the weekend because of a power cut.
ABLE
We .... to watch TV since the weekend because of a power cut.

4 I'm sure those gloves don't belong to Peter because I saw him put his in his bag.
BE
They .... gloves because I saw him put his in his bag.

5 It was a mistake not to phone Granny to tell her we were coming because she wasn't in when we arrived.
SHOULD
We .... Granny to tell her we were coming because she wasn't in when we arrived.

6 I'm sure our new neighbour is famous as I keep seeing a photographer outside the house.
BE
Our new neighbour .... famous as I keep seeing a photographer outside the house.

7 It's possible that my phone fell out of my bag in the changing room.
MIGHT
My phone .... out of my bag in the changing room.

8 When I was little, I could walk on my hands but I can't any more!
ABLE
When I was little, I .... walk on my hands but I can't any more!

Modal verbs

4 Complete each sentence with a word from the box.

> can   can't   might   must   should   shouldn't

1 That .... be Jonnie's coat but I'm not sure. He's got a new one.
2 You .... play volleyball with us if you want.
3 We .... have caught an earlier bus. Then we wouldn't have been so late.
4 There's nobody at home so they .... have gone out somewhere.
5 You .... give people advice you don't follow yourself.
6 You .... take that rucksack into the museum. It's not allowed.

Reading and Use of English Part 2

Common phrases for Use of English Part 2

Complete the sentences with one word.

1 .... from Paolo, nobody in the class had been go-karting before.
2 I started cycling to school in .... to save money.
3 We went camping on holiday this year .... of renting an apartment like we usually do.
4 My friend is known .... Nell although her real name is Ellen.
5 My mum said I can invite .... to 25 friends to my party but no more than that.
6 We can choose to go either to an art gallery next Friday .... to the botanic gardens and do our own drawings.
7 We all have to help at home by doing jobs .... as emptying the dishwasher and putting the rubbish out.
8 Tara is a good friend of .... – I've known her since I was five.

Exam task

For questions 1–8, read the text below and think of the word which best fits each gap. Use only one word in each gap. There is an example at the beginning (0).

Example: 0   BY

A train in a restaurant

Choo Choo Johnny's Eatery was founded **(0)** .... John and Patricia Ethell in Chicago, USA. When their children were little and they used to take them to restaurants, the children got bored quickly and **(1)** .... unable to sit still for longer **(2)** .... a few minutes. So John and Patricia came **(3)** .... with the idea of opening a unique restaurant **(4)** .... would be fun for both adults and kids. **(5)** .... spending months planning it and getting advice on running a restaurant, they finally opened in December 2002. In the restaurant, customers sit on stools and the food is delivered by model trains which run up and down the long table. The waiters are dressed **(6)** .... if they were engineers and there is also a model city with trains going round it. The restaurant has become **(7)** .... of the most popular in Chicago and people travel there from all over the city as **(8)** .... as the surrounding area.

5 LEARNING

Listening Part 2

Exam task

🎧 **06** You will hear a teacher at a secondary school giving some students advice about how to choose a career. For questions 1–10, complete the sentences with a word or short phrase. Play the recording twice.

The teacher tells the students to consider their
(1) .... as well as what they are good at when choosing a career.

The job of (2) .... is given as an example of work involving contact with people.

Joining the (3) .... is said to be suitable for someone good at dealing with serious problems.

The teacher recommends that students make a list of their
(4) .... in a job.

Students are asked to consider whether they want job satisfaction and (5) .... in the longer term.

Once students have decided on a particular job, they should check the (6) .... needed.

Students are warned that if they want to be a
(7) ...., they may need to leave their home area to find work.

The teacher says that (8) .... should not be the students' main motivation at the start of a career.

The teacher mentions being a (9) .... as one example of doing a job involving something you feel passionate about.

The teacher finishes by suggesting that everyone should get some
(10) .... before deciding on a career.

Reading and Use of English Part 7

1 Look at the titles of some summer courses below. What subject does each one concentrate on: film, history, language, science or sport?

Ancient Egypt

The rainforest

Contemporary poets

Fun and fitness

Sea creatures

Inside the human body

A cameraman's view

Storytellers

21st-century space travel

Surf safari

Hollywood greats

A century of food

2 Quickly read the text 'Summer camps'. Are all five texts about the same summer camp? Did the writers all enjoy themselves?

Exam tip ›

Remember to read all the texts quickly first, then go back to Text A. Go through the questions and find which ones match the information in A. Do the same with the other texts.

Exam task

You are going to read a magazine article about students at summer camps. For questions 1–10, choose from the students A–E. The people may be chosen more than once.

Which student

says they now work more efficiently because of the ways of working they learnt?	1
changed their attitude to their work during their stay?	2
found out during their stay what kinds of things they were especially good at?	3
was concerned that they didn't have the right knowledge to carry out a task?	4
was pleased to get some individual attention?	5
is surprised at how much they have been influenced by the other students?	6
appreciated the fact that students were not assessed on what they did?	7
says they found those in charge easy to feel comfortable with?	8
had to rewrite what they did several times after getting feedback?	9
felt the course stood out as being superior to others they had attended?	10

Summer camps

Five students talk about their experiences

A Ryan

I've just got back from two weeks at Pioneer Basketball Camp. I decided to go, thinking it would be just another summer sports camp experience for me but I was truly mistaken as it was really inspiring. When I got there, I realised I was completely unfit. Every morning our coach worked us as hard as he could for three hours straight, then we played a match. On top of that we did activities every evening but they were a great opportunity to make new friends and find out what the organisers were really like. They weren't much older than most of the campers, which made them seem like an older brother or sister.

B Eliza

I was delighted when I learnt that I was one of the selected candidates for the National History Foundation summer school. Hearing my classmates read out details of their history projects inspired me and opened me up to new ideas. The most productive parts, however, and the most fun, were the discussions that took place in my dormitory. The twelve of us commented on each other's work openly, unafraid of making suggestions for improvements where we could. Whether I see them again, or correspond with them for years to come, I'm glad to have met them all. The impact that many of them had on me in such a short time has amazed me and I still think about a lot of the things we talked about.

C Ruby

At SuperScientist Camp, everybody took one key course in science and one they could choose. All of the teachers were specialised in their area and full of energy and fun. You didn't get marks or grades for the courses so there was no stress put on homework or assignments in class, which was great. There are so many little tricks which I picked up that have helped me work faster while improving the quality of my work. Memorising lists of names by singing them as the lyrics of my favourite songs seemed like it wouldn't work, but it did! SuperScientist Camp also helped me to become aware of what my strengths are and how to use them to overcome my weaknesses.

D Ethan

I did a media summer camp where we were able to become journalists. We interviewed people on the street, reported news stories on television and learnt how to write headlines, feature articles and news stories. We had to edit our work over and over and get it looked at by our instructor, who gave us constructive criticism on how to improve it. I'd been very involved on my school magazine for a while but we had to produce a whole newspaper at summer camp. I was nervous that I'd have no idea how to tackle that.

E Alana

Although attending classes was the last thing I'd intended to do with my summer vacation, I was glad to go when it came to it as I was getting bored at home. I learnt lots of tips on how to write really good essays. The writing skills classes especially helped me write with greater confidence. With small classes, we all got a lot of one-to-one teaching which really benefited me. The programme was designed to give us the experience of managing our own schedules. I tried to finish all the essays and assignments early so I could sleep or explore the campus. But after the first week, I told myself to focus and stop avoiding my responsibilities. That was quite a step forward for me.

Vocabulary

Phrasal verbs *get* and *go*

Complete the phrasal verb in each sentence with a preposition from the box. Use your dictionary if you need to.

at	into	over

1 I practised hard because I really wanted to get .... the basketball team.
2 We've moved all the plates to a higher shelf so my baby brother can't get .... them.
3 My sister took ages to get .... the illness she had last summer but she's nearly better now.

away with	round to	out of

4 I thought I'd get .... copying my friend's homework but the teacher noticed.
5 I tried to get .... babysitting tomorrow because I want to see my friends but I have to do it.
6 I never seem to get .... tidying my bedroom because there's always something more interesting to do.

across	to	up

7 I don't know where my dad's got .... He said he'd pick me up at 6.00.
8 I was so angry I got .... and left the room so I wouldn't say something I'd regret.
9 Our geography teacher's so good at getting information .... that we always understand when he explains.

ahead	by	for

10 I'm not sure about trying for a part in the school play but my mum says I should go .... it.
11 People say that time goes .... much faster as you get older but I don't believe it.
12 The art teacher told us to go .... and start painting as soon as we were ready.

off	on	through

13 My sister went .... talking even though nobody was listening to her.
14 I went .... all my pockets but I couldn't find the key.
15 I used to love tomatoes but I've gone .... them recently.

Grammar

wish, *if only* and preferences

1 Look at these sentences. Is the writer referring to past, present or future events?

1 I wish I could go to France this summer. ....
2 I wish I hadn't eaten so much ice cream. ....
3 I'd rather you didn't sit at this table. ....
4 I wish this bag wasn't so heavy. ....
5 If only I'd had time to finish my homework yesterday. (But I didn't.) ....
6 If only Jane would lend me her necklace for the party tomorrow. (But I know she won't.) ....

2 Now complete these sentences with the verb in the correct tense.

1 I wish I .... (finish) my essay yesterday, but I didn't have time.
2 If only I .... (go) to bed early yesterday, I'd have felt better today.
3 I'd rather we .... (see) the film at 6.00 if that's OK with you.
4 Anna wishes she .... (live) in Australia, where it's warm.
5 I'd rather you .... (not talk) while I'm trying to work.
6 If only my parents .... (let) me go travelling when I leave school!
7 I wish I .... (not lose) my sunglasses yesterday.
8 I'd rather we .... (sit) together on the plane as it's a long flight.
9 I wish my school .... (not be) so far away from where I live.
10 When the others all went in the sea, Matt wished he .... (bring) his swimming things.

Conditionals, wishes and preferences

3 Complete the second sentence so it has a similar meaning to the first sentence, using the word given. Use between two and five words.

1 It wasn't Susie's fault, so I shouldn't have raised my voice at her.
SHOUTED
I wish that .... Susie, because it wasn't her fault.

2 I think it's better if you catch the early bus.
RATHER
I .... the early bus.

3 I'll clear up after dinner, but I need to call Sam first.
CAN
I'll clear up after dinner provided that .... I do it.

4 Peter missed the bus, so he had to cycle.
HAVE
If Peter hadn't missed the bus, he .... cycle.

5 I didn't succeed in getting into the school tennis team as I had wanted.
WOULD
I had .... into the school tennis team, but I didn't.

6 It could be cold at night, so take some warm clothes with you.
CASE
Take some warm clothes with you .... cold at night.

7 I won't be able to go to the party if my parents don't agree to it.
UNLESS
I won't be able to go to the party .... to it.

8 I'll play squash with Antonio tonight unless we get too much homework.
GIVEN
I'll play squash with Antonio tonight if .... too much homework.

Reading and Use of English Part 1
Exam task

For questions 1–8, read the text below and decide which answer (A, B, C or D) best fits each gap. There is an example at the beginning (0).

Example:
0 **A** belonged   **B** joined   **C** located   **D** linked

A travelling school

Alexandra Lavrillier grew up in France, but always felt she **(0)** .... in the far north of our world. She now spends **(1)** .... all the year in Siberia, where winter temperatures can drop to below -40°C. It all started in 1994 when Alexandra went on an expedition to Yakutia in Siberia, **(2)** .... by several French photographers. There she met the Evenk people, whose **(3)** .... of life means they are constantly travelling around the region. The Evenk children **(4)** .... went to schools far from their families. Alexandra realised that it was crucial that a travelling school was **(5)** .... up in order to **(6)** .... the survival of the Evenk culture. The first one started in 2006. Now the children are taught by teachers who travel from one camp to another, with the time spent at each camp **(7)** .... on the pupils' needs. The children have the **(8)** .... to study their traditions and language as well as all the usual subjects, including technology.

1	**A** quite	**B** about	**C** rather	**D** almost
2	**A** accompanied	**B** attended	**C** participated	**D** contributed
3	**A** method	**B** means	**C** way	**D** system
4	**A** however	**B** whereas	**C** nevertheless	**D** therefore
5	**A** got	**B** set	**C** made	**D** turned
6	**A** ensure	**B** check	**C** prove	**D** emphasise
7	**A** according	**B** corresponding	**C** depending	**D** associating
8	**A** circumstance	**B** occasion	**C** prospect	**D** chance

Listening Part 4

Read the exam task and questions quickly. Which of these things do you think you will hear about?

> birds   cinema   famous buildings   food
> history   music   plants   shops   sport
> the environment

Exam task

🎧 **07** You will hear an English girl called Annie talking about a trip her family made to Australia. For questions 1–7, choose the best answer (**A, B or C**). Play the recording twice.

1   What was Annie's first impression of Australia?
  A Wild animals are kept as pets there.
  B Tourists are frightened by the wildlife.
  C Australians live in close contact with nature.

2   What did Annie dislike about the Blue Mountains National Park?
  A the pollution in some of the water
  B the lighting of some of the natural features
  C the long distances she had to walk

3   What does Annie say about the activities at Tobruk sheep station?
  A The sheepdogs are entertaining to watch.
  B The past is brought to life effectively.
  C The workers have fantastic riding skills.

4   What surprised Annie about her overnight stay at the sheep station?
  A how early she had to get up
  B how quiet she found it
  C how many stars she saw

5   What problem did Annie have while surfing?
  A She had trouble keeping her balance.
  B She swallowed a lot of sea water.
  C She hit herself on the board.

6   Which tourist activity in Sydney did everyone in Annie's family enjoy?
  A the tour of the Opera House
  B the exhibits at the Maritime Museum
  C the view from the Harbour Bridge

7   What advice does Annie give about visiting Australia?
  A Try to visit as many areas as you can.
  B Make sure you explore a reef.
  C Avoid the desert caves in summer.

Vocabulary

Phrasal verbs

1   Some phrasal verbs have more than one meaning. Underline the phrasal verb in each pair and then choose the meaning, A or B, which matches each one.

1   The band's new album came out yesterday.
2   The sun finally came out after days of rain.

  A to appear in the sky
  B to become available to buy or to see.

3   She ran so fast I couldn't keep up with her.
4   My father is always looking at the Internet because he likes to keep up with the latest news.

  A to move at the same speed as someone
  B to understand or deal with something which is changing very fast

5   I made a cake for the school party but it didn't turn out very well.
6   Thousands of people turned out to see the princess open the new town hall.

  A to go to watch an event or take part in it
  B to have a particular result, especially an unexpected one

2 Now complete these sentences with the verbs from Exercise 1.

1 There are so many new developments in the computer industry that it's hard to .... them.
2 Our exam results .... last Friday.
3 The painting I did .... much better than I expected.
4 I'm looking forward to seeing the new James Bond film when it ....
5 We could hear a strange noise, which .... to be our neighbour practising his new saxophone!
6 My new shoes were hurting and I couldn't .... the others because I was walking so slowly.

Grammar

too and enough

1 ⊙ Correct the mistakes in these sentences written by exam candidates.

1 Was the film enough exciting for you?
2 It's very late and we are so tired to eat.
3 We tried to light a candle but the wind was to strong.
4 The streets are dirty because money isn't enough to clean them.
5 I think we would be so exhausted to enjoy the wonderful view if we cycled.
6 The month of May is best for holidays because the weather isn't hot enough.

so and such

2 ⊙ Choose so or such in these sentences written by exam candidates.

1 Louisa will enjoy the art class because she's so / such good at drawing.
2 The organisers of the camp were so / such nice people.
3 I wonder how top models stay looking so / such perfect?
4 We had so / such a laugh when we went to the funfair.
5 We have so / such good memories of our holidays with you.
6 There were so / such many things to do in Berlin we didn't know where to go first.

Reading and Use of English Part 2
Exam task

For questions 1–8, read the text below and think of the word which best fits each gap. Use only one word in each gap. There is an example at the beginning (0).

Example: 0   AGO

Chimpanzees

Humans and chimpanzees are thought to share a common ancestor who lived four to eight million years **(0)** .... Chimpanzees live mostly in the African rainforest but they can also live in drier areas with fewer trees as **(1)** .... as they can access the forest for shelter and food. **(2)** .... they normally walk on four legs, chimpanzees can also stand and walk upright. Their arms and legs are **(3)** .... strong that they can swing easily from branch to branch in the trees, **(4)** .... they do most of their eating. They have **(5)** .... varied diet that includes hundreds of different foods.

In addition, chimpanzees are **(6)** .... of the few animal species that use tools. They shape and use sticks to get insects **(7)** .... of the trees, smash open tasty nuts with stones and use leaves as if they were sponges to soak up drinking water. Chimpanzees can even **(8)** .... taught to use some basic human sign language.

Reading and Use of English Part 6

Read the text very quickly and answer these general questions. Don't worry about the gaps in the text.

1 How did 'Plant for the Planet' start?
2 What has the boy achieved?

Exam task

You are going to read a newspaper article about a German boy. Six sentences have been removed from the article. Choose from the sentences **A–G** the one which fits each gap (1–6). There is one extra sentence which you do not need to use.

The tree planter

A boy who started planting trees in Germany has become an international hero.

At the age of nine, Felix Finkbeiner set up an organisation called 'Plant for the Planet', whose aim is to plant one million trees in each country of the world. It now exists in more than 130 countries worldwide and there is a Children's Coordination Council made up of young people who organise plantings and give lectures.

It all started when Felix had to give a presentation at school about climate change. He looked for information on the Internet and was inspired by a woman who had planted 30 million trees in Africa. Her work made him realise how much could be achieved starting from nothing. **1** [ ] The talk was so well received that it was suggested he talked to other schools. He started getting calls from students who wanted to join in and others offered help in building a website. The first tree was planted and 'Plant for the Planet' was launched.

There was a lot to do so Felix asked his parents if he could employ someone to help if he could find the money to pay them. He contacted Toyota, the large car manufacturers, asking for support. **2** [ ] Once he had received the money, Felix was able to deliver his climate-change talk to more and more people.

Six months after the planting of the first tree, Felix gave a talk to a local club of business people. In the audience was the Chief Executive Officer of Toyota Germany, who wanted to hear what his money was being spent on. **3** [ ] This was to talk to that year's annual meeting of German Toyota car dealers. The participants were so interested in the idea that they donated €11,000 to 'Plant for the Planet'. Suddenly the project spread nationally.

Felix invited newspaper and TV journalists to a press conference to announce that 50,000 trees had been planted in Germany. His parents warned him that very few journalists might come. **4** [ ] As a result, Felix and his family realised what a big success this could all be. He has since given hundreds of speeches, encouraging children around the world to plant trees, think about climate change and to act responsibly.

Felix's parents were always determined, however, that their child's feet would stay firmly on the ground. They insist that their family home was very ordinary and that their aim was never to make Felix and his sisters special; that it all came from Felix himself rather than from them. **5** [ ] This was because of a concern about how it would all affect his schoolwork. But Felix came through it all without any problems.

There is actually nothing new in the facts and figures about climate change which Felix put forward. When he is talking about other topics he sounds like any other young person. **6** [ ] He turns into the most confident public speaker. But whatever he does in the rest of his life, he has already achieved more than most of us ever do.

A   But once he gets started on climate issues, a change comes over him.

B   Indeed, his ambitions continued to expand.

C   It was unusual for them to receive such a request but they agreed to help.

D   It gave him the idea that children could do something similar.

E   In fact, they were always likely to hold him back rather than push him forward.

F   But it turned out to be packed and his picture was on TV screens and in newspapers around the country.

G   So impressed was he that he gave Felix an unusual invitation for someone of his age.

Grammar

Countable and uncountable nouns

1   Some uncountable nouns are used with other words to refer to quantity, e.g. we say *a slice of bread*. Match a quantity word in A with an uncountable word in B.

A		B
bar		advice
breath		cheese
can		chocolate
flash		toothpaste
item	of	rain
means		lightning
piece		clothing
shower		fresh air
slice		transport
tube		soup

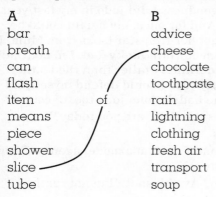

2   Complete these sentences with the expressions above.

1   Mum asked me to go to the shop and buy a .... to heat up at lunchtime.
2   I was in the bathroom brushing my teeth when I dropped the .... on the floor.
3   A huge .... lit up the sky as the storm started.
4   If I've been studying all day, I like to go for a walk and get a .... before dinner.
5   I made a tasty sandwich for lunch using brown bread, a .... and some salad.
6   Bicycles are probably the most popular .... in Amsterdam.
7   A swimming costume is the most important .... to pack for a holiday in a hot country.
8   There was a .... as I was walking to school and I got soaked through.
9   I was so hungry that I ate a whole .... on the way home from school.
10   My grandfather said the best .... he ever received was never to lose your temper.

PEOPLE AND STYLE

Reading and Use of English Part 5

Look at the picture. What are the girls doing? Where are they? Do people do this in your country?

Exam task

You are going to read an extract from a novel. For questions 1–6, choose the answer (**A**, **B**, **C** or **D**) which you think fits best according to the text.

My sister Ava and I were busking: playing music in the street for money.

'Are you sure this is working?' I mutter, as Ava puffs her way through the final chorus of the Beatles song *Yellow Submarine*.

'We're fantastic. Trust me.'

Trouble is, I don't. The last time I trusted my older sister was in primary school, when she assured me that it was normal to wear a Buzz Lightyear costume (complete with wings) to gym club if you accidentally left your sports clothes at your granny's. The teacher made me do the whole class in that costume. Ava laughs whenever she thinks of it. Some memories stay with you forever. 'Jesse's cousin got fifty pounds last week,' she says, encouragingly.

'What, Jesse's cousin, the classical violinist?'

'Uh-huh.'

'Who's in an orchestra?'

'Well, yes,' Ava admits. 'But she was busking in Truro, which is miles from anywhere. And look at us.' I look at us. Location-wise, we're perfect: in the heart of London's West End, surrounded by Saturday shoppers taking advantage of some early summer sun. If we were Ava's boyfriend's cousin, we'd probably make a fortune. But I bet she wasn't playing *Easy Beatles Tunes for Beginners*. And I bet she wasn't accompanied by a girl who only took up the tambourine that morning, like I did. 'There's a guy down the street who seems to be watching us. Over there, see? He might give us a pound or something if we're lucky.'

Ava sighs and looks tired for a moment. 'Let's give them *Hey Jude*. My last performance "had to be heard to be believed", remember?'

I smile. I do indeed remember that quote from the school newsletter last Christmas. I'm not sure they meant it the way she took it, though.

Meanwhile, the guy down the street is slowly heading in our direction. It suddenly occurs to me that he might be a plainclothes policeman, if plainclothes policemen wear leather jackets and carry orange backpacks. Maybe we're not allowed to play here and he's about to arrest us. Or worse, he could be a kidnapper. Thank goodness I did judo in my last year of primary school. And for once, my height could be useful. While Ava got her film-star looks from Mum, I got all my looks from our tall, lanky dad. I'm not Dad's height yet, but I'm definitely taller than the leather jacket guy. I'm pretty sure I could defend myself, if I had to. As long as he hadn't done judo too, of course.

'Hi, girls,' the man says. 'How are you today?'

'Fine,' Ava answers.

'My name's Simon and I'm from a model agency. D'you mind if I take a picture?'

'Oh, I don't think so,' Ava blushes. 'I'm not really—'

'I meant you, actually,' Simon says, gazing past her.

Ava's watching me now. Come to think of it, Simon's definitely looking in my direction. But that can't be right. I stare back at him, confused.

'I've been watching you and you're amazing. Have you thought about modelling?'

What? Amazing? Me? Modelling? No.

Suddenly I feel dizzy. This must be some sort of prank. I assume we're being filmed. Is Ava part of it? She looks as puzzled as I feel. Why is Simon talking to me, when the gorgeous one with the film-star face is standing right beside him?

I guess I'm supposed to say something, but my mouth has dried up. I shake my head.

'You should consider it,' he goes on. He feels in the pocket of his trendy black jeans and hands me a card. 'Tell your parents, too.'

1 Why does the writer mention what happened at the gym?
   A to demonstrate that she has an excellent memory for past events
   B to suggest her sister has a different approach to life from herself
   C to explain why she has given in to her sister's wishes
   D to show why she no longer believes what her sister says

2 The writer doesn't think they should compare themselves with Jesse's cousin because of
   A the music they've chosen to play.
   B the kinds of shoppers in the streets.
   C their level of experience.
   D their present location.

3 How does the writer react to the man's approach?
   A She wishes she were taller and stronger.
   B She thinks of a way of handling a possible situation.
   C Her suspicions about him are confirmed.
   D His appearance makes it obvious to her who he is.

4 What does 'a prank' mean in line 62?
   A an experiment
   B a shock
   C a disagreement
   D a trick

5 What does 'it' refer to in 'You should consider it' in line 69?
   A having her picture taken
   B being a model
   C being filmed
   D saying something

6 What do we find out about the writer in this extract?
   A She is jealous of her sister's optimistic nature.
   B She isn't sensitive to other people's needs.
   C She gets easily discouraged when things go wrong.
   D She doesn't have much confidence in herself.

Vocabulary

People: Useful expressions

Complete this word puzzle, using the clues below.

Across
1 I was full so I shook my .... when Mum asked if I wanted any more cake.
3 Frank is so .... of himself, he assumes everything will always work out all right.
4 When I first met Charlie I had the .... he was very shy but in fact he's not.
7 My friend is so funny to be with – he has a great sense of ....
8 I knew I had to tell the truth so I took a deep .... and began.
9 The other children made .... of Mark because he had an unusual accent.
10 My dad lost his .... and got really angry when someone scratched his car.
11 I couldn't believe my .... when I heard I'd got first prize.
12 My friends played a .... on me and hid my shoes after our swimming lesson.

Down
2 It was a huge .... when Dad said we couldn't go sailing because he had to work.
5 I'm .... of everyone telling me what to do all the time.
6 It really gets on my .... when someone sings along to the music they're listening to on their headphones.
9 I made a .... of myself in the shop when I complained about getting the wrong change and then I found I'd made a mistake.

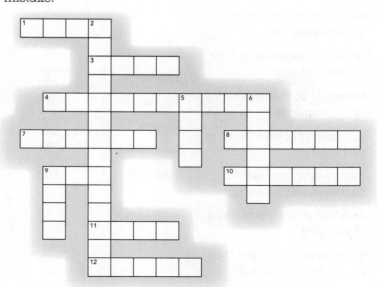

A

B

C

Listening Part 3

1 You are going to hear about some fun family outings. What are they? Match three of the activities with the pictures.

> visiting a sea life centre   watching horse racing
> climbing in the tree tops   quad biking
> visiting a tropical rainforest   horse riding
> going on a climbing wall

2 Have you been on any outings like these? Did you enjoy them?

Exam task

🎧 **08** You will hear five short extracts in which people are talking about outings they went on with their families. For questions 1–5, choose from the list (**A–H**) how each speaker felt about the outing. Use the letters only once. There are three extra letters which you do not need to use. Play the recording twice.

A pleased by the range of activities

B excited at the chance to acquire a new skill

C relieved to be involved in an outdoor activity

D impressed by the personality of the instructor

E surprised at being allowed to participate

F glad to have had their questions well answered

G satisfied at doing something challenging

H encouraged to increase their knowledge of a subject

Speaker 1 ☐ 1

Speaker 2 ☐ 2

Speaker 3 ☐ 3

Speaker 4 ☐ 4

Speaker 5 ☐ 5

Grammar

to-infinitive and *-ing* form

1 Are the verbs in the box followed by the *to*-infinitive or *-ing* form? Write them in the correct column in the table below.

> aim   arrange   avoid   consider   decide
> deserve   imagine   involve   manage   mention
> offer   practise   pretend   refuse   suggest

to-infinitive	*-ing*

2 Now complete these sentences with a verb from the table. Not all the verbs are used.

1 David absolutely .... to make any changes to the original plan, although we asked him to.

2 There were big traffic jams around the airport, but we .... to catch our plane.

3 We all thought Tina .... to win the swimming prize because she had trained hard all year.

4 When I walked into the room, my little sister .... to be asleep.

5 My older brother is a good cook, but he always tries to .... clearing up.

6 I .... studying Spanish, but in the end I took up German.

Reported speech

3 Complete the first gap in the sentences with a reporting verb from the box. Complete the second gap with reported speech. Use each reporting verb once only.

agree apologise ask enquire
explain tell warn wonder

1 'Yeah, of course I'll go to the cinema with you.'
My sister .... to .... to the cinema with me.
2 'Will you help me finish my project later?'
My friend .... if .... him to finish his project later.
3 'This is how you must do the equation.' The teacher .... how .... the equation.
4 'When does the next train for London leave?'
The passenger .... when the next train for London ....
5 'Don't be late for the exam!'
Our teacher .... us not .... late for the exam.
6 'The answer is 24.'
Anna .... me the answer .... 24.
7 'Sorry, but I really can't agree with what you are saying.'
My grandmother .... for not being able to agree with what I .... saying.
8 'Did I say something that offended Molly?'
I .... whether I .... something that had offended Molly.

Vocabulary

Shopping

Here are some notices you might see in shops. Complete them with these words.

bargain catalogues debit exchange
goods guarantee sale stock

1 If we don't have what you want in .... , take one of our .... and order online.
2 Pick up a .... in our .... , which begins Monday. Everything reduced.
3 We offer a one-year .... on all electrical ....
4 You can return items for .... or refund within 28 days. Money is refunded to your credit or .... card.

Reading and Use of English Part 4

Exam task

For questions 1–6, complete the second sentence so that it has a similar meaning to the first sentence, using the word given. **Do not change the word given.** You must use between two and five words, including the word given.

Here is an example (0):

0 My friend said I could borrow his bike if I took care of it.
LONG
My friend said I could borrow his bike as ...._long as I looked_.... after it.

1 I thought I was winning the race but Frank overtook me at the end.
BY
I thought I was winning the race but I .... at the end.

2 The teacher asked if anyone knew where her laptop lead had gone.
MY
The teacher asked: '............................ laptop lead has gone?'

3 I did the washing-up yesterday so I think it's Luke's turn to do it today.
SHOULD
I think .... the washing-up today because I did it yesterday.

4 I didn't phone you because I left my mobile at home.
HAVE
If I hadn't left my mobile at home, I .... you.

5 Before I'm allowed to go out with my friends on Saturdays, my mum makes me tidy my room.
LET
My mum .... go out with my friends on Saturdays until I've tidied my room.

6 The man spoke so quietly that nobody could hear him.
HAD
The man .... voice that nobody could hear him.

Reading and Use of English Part 6

1 You are going to read an article about sleep. Read these statements and decide if they are true or false.

1 Twelve per cent of people dream only in black and white.
2 A short sleep in the daytime helps your memory.
3 The average dream lasts between 30 minutes and an hour.
4 Approximately one third of your life is spent sleeping.
5 The record for the longest period without sleep is seven days, 21 hours and 40 minutes.
6 Teenagers need on average about 10.5 hours' sleep a night.

2 Check your answers at the end of the book.

Exam task

You are going to read a newspaper article about when we sleep. Six sentences have been removed from the article. Choose from the sentences **A–G** the one which fits each gap (**1–6**). There is one extra sentence which you do not need to use.

> **Exam tip ⟩**
>
> Remember to read the text once for general understanding, then read it again more slowly, choosing one of the sentences A–G for each gap. Read the text again and check the sentences you've chosen fit each gap.

Bring back the night

Our lives are ruled by time and we use time to tell us what to do. But the digital alarm clock that wakes us in the morning or the wristwatch that tells us we are late for supper are unnatural clocks. Fixed within our genes, and those of almost all life on Earth, are the instructions for a biological clock. This marks the passage of approximately 24 hours and dominates everything we do. Even our ability to learn and do well in exams is affected by it.

Biological clocks or "circadian clocks" help time our sleep patterns. **1** ☐ It is therefore these internal clocks which are used to anticipate the differing demands of the 24-hour day and adapt our physiology and behaviour in advance of changing conditions.

Before we go to bed, our body temperature drops, our blood pressure decreases, and tiredness increases. **2** ☐ Few of us appreciate this internal world, however. We are drawn by an apparent freedom to sleep, work, eat, drink or travel when we want.

Body clocks differ between people. If you are alert in the mornings and go to bed early, you are a morning "lark", but if you hate mornings and want to keep going through the night, you are a night "owl". **3** ☐ In our first decade, we tend to wake early, but by the time we are teenagers, bedtimes and getting-up times become later and later.

This habit of getting up later continues until we are about 20 years old. **4** ☐ By the age of 55–60 we are getting up as early as we did when we were 10. This could explain why young adults really do have a problem getting up in the morning. Teenagers show both delayed sleep and lack of sleep because they are going to bed late but still having to get up early in the morning to go to school.

These real biological effects have been largely ignored in terms of the time structure imposed upon teenagers at school. Paul Kelly, the headmaster of Monkseaton High School near Newcastle, has adopted a later start to the school day and this is having a positive impact. [5] Ironically though, while young adults tend to improve their performance across the day, their older teachers show a decline in performance over the same period.

We humans have welcomed the freedom to do what we want, when we want. Our 24/7 society has invaded the night, an apparent victory of civilisation over nature. [6] Disrupting sleep and circadian rhythm actually has a negative effect on our brains and that drives many of us to substitute the rhythm normally imposed by internal time with coffee and sugary snacks to give us energy and keep us awake. But we have not achieved freedom, we have just created a 24/7 timetable which we cannot keep to without damaging our health.

A By contrast, as dawn approaches, our bodies get themselves ready for increased activity when we wake.

B There are fewer absences and improved results.

C These include, in fact, increased errors, poor memory, reduced mental and physical reaction times and reduced motivation.

D At this point there is a change towards earlier sleep and waking times.

E But the reality is that our society is replacing a biological order, developed over millions of years of evolution, with a false impression.

F These differences are partly laid down within our genes but they also change significantly as we get older.

G They also control our levels of attention, mood, physical strength, blood pressure and much more.

Vocabulary

The human body

Which words are connected? Match each word in Column A with a word in Column B.

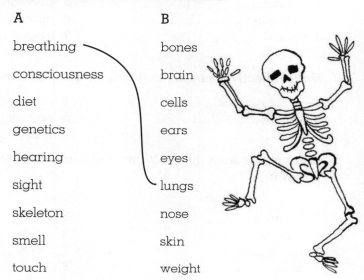

A	B
breathing	bones
consciousness	brain
diet	cells
genetics	ears
hearing	eyes
sight	lungs
skeleton	nose
smell	skin
touch	weight

Grammar

Relative clauses

Correct these mistakes made by exam candidates.

1 The book, that I read it yesterday, was very interesting.
2 Paul lives in the house over there who it has a red front door.
3 I didn't understand everything what the teacher said in maths today.
4 I'd like to meet people which have the same interests as me.
5 The star had been replaced by another actor, that didn't have his talent.
6 I have been to the United States twice, that enabled me to improve my English.
7 There was a very high window in the room where it was almost impossible to open.
8 I don't know the name of the boy whose sitting in the front row.
9 At the zoo, I took pictures of animals who are in danger.
10 The teacher said we could leave early, that we all thought was a good idea.

Reading and Use of English Part 3

Word building: Adjectives ending in *-ic/-ive* and irregular nouns

1 Make adjectives ending in *-ive*, *-sive*, or *-tive* from the words below.

1 attract ....
2 communicate ....
3 create ....
4 decide ....

5 decorate ....
6 effect ....
7 extend ....
8 impress ....

9 offend ....
10 produce ....
11 progress ....
12 protect ....

2 Make adjectives ending in *-ic*, *-tic* or *-istic* from the words below.

1 art ....
2 athlete ....
3 atom ....

4 economy ....
5 enthusiasm ....
6 history ....

7 pessimism ....
8 real ....

3 Make nouns from the following verbs and adjectives. They are all fairly common but don't follow a regular pattern.

Verbs

1 believe ....
2 choose ....
3 die ....
4 give ....

5 know ....
6 marry ....
7 prove ....
8 laugh ....

9 see ....
10 speak ....
11 think ....
12 succeed ....

Adjectives

13 free ....
14 long ....

15 high ....
16 proud ....

17 strong ....
18 wide ....

Exam task

For questions 1–8, read the text below. Use the word given in capitals at the end of some of the lines to form a word that fits in the gap **in the same line**. There is an example at the beginning (**0**).

Example: 0   *TRULY*

THE NIGHT SKY

A child born today in Europe has only a one in ten chance of ever
seeing a **(0)** .... dark sky. Thousands of stars which were   **TRUE**
once **(1)** .... to the naked eye can no longer be seen. This   **VISION**
is because of the **(2)** .... of artificial lights. In cities, people   **BRIGHT**
usually see fewer than 500 stars, whereas in really dark places there
can be a **(3)** .... display of around 15,000 stars. People now   **DRAMA**
travel to ideal **(4)** .... like New Zealand and the Atacama   **LOCATE**
Desert especially to look at the night sky. In these remote areas there
is a very **(5)** .... view of the sky that was available to everyone   **IMPRESS**
before the invention of **(6)** .... Although the constant light   **ELECTRIC**
in our cities is **(7)** .... for people who would like to see the   **CONVENIENCE**
stars there is a more serious problem. The fact that it is never dark is
(8) .... to animals and birds as they confuse night and day   **HARM**
and sleep and eat at the wrong times.

Listening Part 1

Exam tip ›

Before you do the exam task, read the questions and answers quickly.

Which question(s) ask(s) about
a) feelings or opinions?
b) the main topic?
c) what the speaker is trying to do?

Exam task

🎧 **09** You will hear people talking in eight different situations. For questions 1–8, choose the best answer (**A**, **B** or **C**). Play the recording twice.

1 You hear two friends talking.
What are they talking about?
A a book
B a film
C a TV programme

2 You hear a boy talking about a new video game.
What impressed him about the game?
A It had great graphics.
B It made him think hard.
C It had exciting action shots.

3 You hear a teacher talking to his students.
What does he want to do?
A ask them to prepare some questions
B inform them that a speaker is coming
C get them to reorganise the room

4 You hear a girl leaving a phone message for her mother.
The girl is calling
A to ask for a lift home.
B to change a plan.
C to explain what she's doing.

5 You hear a girl telling a friend about her new art teacher.
What does she like about the teacher?
A She is very friendly with all the students.
B She allows the students to develop their own style.
C She gives students ideas by showing them famous pictures.

6 You hear a career adviser talking to a group of students.
What advice is she giving?
A Get a broad range of qualifications if you can.
B Choose the subjects that you are best at.
C Take qualifications useful in a particular career.

7 You hear two students talking at school.
What has the girl enjoyed about her day?
A doing some chemistry work
B designing scenery for a play
C studying a chapter in a novel

8 You hear a boy starting to give a talk to his class.
The boy wants to explain
A how he chose the subject for his talk.
B how he is going to organise his talk.
C how he found the information for his talk.

Vocabulary

Computers

Match the (halves of) words in Column A with those in Column B to make ten words related to computers. Then find the words in the wordsearch square below (→↓).

A
back book down hard log pass re spread up web

B
sheet date cam drive up word mark load start in

F	H	K	P	E	Q	V	N	L	X	A	W	B	F	D
S	Y	U	G	K	U	R	T	M	Z	V	B	O	O	D
G	N	H	H	L	U	A	X	H	J	R	S	O	K	W
H	K	R	W	S	P	Z	O	I	A	E	L	K	Y	U
S	P	R	E	A	D	S	H	E	E	T	W	M	T	P
C	A	F	B	F	A	F	Y	U	D	A	F	A	E	Q
V	S	Z	C	X	T	V	A	S	F	T	G	R	S	N
J	S	I	A	C	E	Q	S	T	B	A	C	K	U	P
F	W	J	M	Y	T	O	R	B	X	X	T	I	C	R
A	O	K	M	J	S	G	R	E	S	T	A	R	T	I
E	R	H	D	L	A	L	E	M	G	B	U	O	B	S
Y	D	O	W	N	L	O	A	D	H	H	A	P	H	T
R	L	D	B	M	I	G	P	H	I	O	E	M	K	E
H	A	R	D	D	R	I	V	E	L	Z	C	D	M	A
C	N	T	P	B	K	N	G	L	N	D	V	A	A	P

Unit 1

Writing Part 1: Essay

1 Complete the paragraph below about family celebrations using the linking phrases in the box. Use each phrase only once.

> as for   for example   for that reason   in contrast
> though

> My family is very varied in age. **(1)** .... organizing an activity to celebrate a birthday or special occasion that everyone enjoys is, in general, rather difficult. **(2)** .... , my little sister, who is only four, loves playing party games. **(3)** .... my big brother, who is twenty, he thinks it's exciting to go into town with his friends and celebrate there. **(4)** .... , my grandparents, who are in their seventies, really prefer a quiet evening dinner by candlelight. We all get on well **(5)** .... , so that helps!

2 Look at the linking phrases 1–10. When would you use them in an essay? Write them in boxes A–D.

1 owing to
2 with the aim of
3 therefore
4 moreover
5 due to
6 furthermore
7 in order to
8 with a view to
9 as a result
10 in addition

A to express a purpose	B to add information

C to give a reason	D to explain a result

3 Decide which phrases from Exercise 2 fit grammatically in these sentences. There is usually more than one answer.

1 The party was cancelled .... the heavy snow that fell during the night.
2 My town is holding a dance this spring to celebrate its 500th anniversary. .... , a huge firework display will be organised in the summer.
3 The council has started collecting money .... raising enough to pay for the display.
4 Two of the children in my class went to Spain .... meet their Spanish cousins.
5 The school has two new language teachers. .... , my friends and I can now do classes in Japanese and Italian.

4 Choose the correct linking phrase.

1 My family arrived late for the play *owing to / therefore* the heavy traffic.
2 My little sister wears her school uniform all the time, *with the aim of / in order to* impress her friends.
3 The concert hall has recently been extended, *with a view to / in addition* adding more seats.
4 Several members of the basketball team were ill and *as a result / moreover* we lost the final.
5 My older sister applied to university, *due to / with the aim of* studying to be a pharmacist.
6 The council has opened a new theatre. *Furthermore / Owing to*, they are planning to build a new cinema.
7 My friend Susanna has worked hard at school this year; *therefore / due to* she has passed all her exams.
8 Martin's taken up tennis this year, *moreover / with a view to* getting really fit.
9 I'm studying for a piano exam this year. *In order to / In addition*, I'm learning how to play the guitar.
10 *With the aim of / Due to* his brilliant performance at the school concert, my brother was selected for a local orchestra.

There's a boat at last. I might be rescued.

SOME TIME EARLIER...

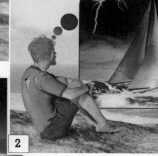

Unit 2

Writing Part 2: Story

1 Read this first sentence of a Part 2 story and answer the questions.

> As he looked out to sea and saw them coming towards him, John knew that he would be all right.
>
> Your story must include:
> - a boat
> - a rescue

  1 Where was John?
  2 What do you think had happened to him?

2 The pictures on the right tell John's story. Decide what is happening in each one.

3 Read the paragraphs. Put them in the correct order by matching them with the pictures. Don't worry about the gaps.

1 ..E..   2 ....   3 ....   4 ....   5 ....

Who is it?

A Fortunately, John just .... (have) time to send one radio message before the boat .... (sink). Then he .... (be) in the water, swimming towards the beach.

B John still remembered very clearly that horrible night when everything .... (go) wrong. He .... (take) part in a round-the-world race, sailing alone on his yacht, when a huge wave .... (hit) it.

C John knew then that he could survive, so he just .... (have to) wait and hope. He had no idea exactly how much time .... (pass) when he noticed the boat .... (change) direction and was now heading towards him. Just a few more moments and he would be safe. Who .... (come) to rescue him?

D When John finally reached the shore, he .... (realise) at once that he was on a small desert island. Fortunately, there .... (be) a small stream with fresh water, and John soon .... (find) some trees with coconuts and fruit on, too. He also .... (learn) very quickly how to catch fish.

E A boat was sailing near to the island at last. It .... (be) such a long wait, John .... (almost give up).

4 Now complete the story by writing the verbs in the gaps, in the correct form.

5 The story has a very open ending: the reader has to guess who was coming to rescue John. Who do you think it was?

  A the navy   **B** his family   **C** some pirates
  D another sailor in the race   **E** a cruise ship

6 Complete the sentences with a preposition, adverb or conjunction from the box.

> after ago before during for
> since until when

  1 It was not .... another boat came by that John was rescued.
  2 John was rescued .... spending several weeks on the island.
  3 John's boat sank about two years ....
  4 It was .... a round-the-world race that John's boat sank.
  5 John has not taken part in a sailing race .... he was rescued.
  6 It was a long time .... John was finally rescued.
  7 John has decided not to go to sea again .... a long time.
  8 .... he found some water, John knew he could survive.

Writing Part 2: Review

1 Match the kinds of review (1–6) with groups of words that might appear in them (A–F).

1 album .... 2 book .... 3 concert .... 4 film .... 5 play .... 6 TV programme ....

A director make-up acting stage costume parts
B star new series drama viewers channel
C singer guitar riff audience band keyboard live performance
D set location action shots special effects cameraman/woman stunts
E songs lyrics lead guitarist vocal range tracks ballad
F characters opening chapter author plot description narrative

2 Complete the book review with phrases A–H. Then write out the review, dividing it into four paragraphs.

A which make you think
B what would have happened
C you are entertained
D and more importantly
E as a result
F in my opinion
G make you feel as if
H a book you really must read

I'd say that *The Hound of the Baskervilles* is **(1)** .... The story takes place in a lonely and deserted place and the descriptions of it **(2)** .... you are really there. I found the book quite frightening in places and, **(3)** .... of that, I decided never to read it late at night! Yet **(4)** .... because the writer builds up the atmosphere so skilfully. At times things happen **(5)** .... that the hound, a giant dog that is supposed to haunt the area, is supernatural. In fact it is not, **(6)** .... , this myth of a ghostly hound is being used as a way to frighten and kill people so that someone can inherit a large amount of money. The famous detective Sherlock Holmes eventually finds the truth with the help of his good friend Dr Watson, and you wonder **(7)** .... if they had not gone to investigate. In conclusion, I would say that, **(8)** .... , *The Hound of the Baskervilles* is an outstanding book. Once you start reading it, you won't be able to put it down!

3 Some reviews contain negative adjectives as well as positive ones. The adjectives below often appear in reviews. Write P for positive or N for negative by each one.

awful .... brilliant .... dreadful .... dull .... entertaining .... fascinating ....
fantastic .... horrible .... intelligent .... stupid .... terrible .... wonderful ....

4 Choose the correct adjectives in this review.

Everyone had told me that the new series on Channel 4 called *Family Time* was absolutely (1) *awful / brilliant* and that I had to watch it. So on Saturday evening my sister and I sat down with some popcorn to watch what we hoped would be a really (2) *entertaining / terrible* new show. But it was just (3) *dreadful / fantastic*. The characters were (4) *fascinating / dull* and the plot was really (5) *intelligent / stupid*. The only thing I liked about the programme was the hero – we both thought he was (6) *horrible / wonderful*!

Writing Part 2: Letter and email

1 Decide which of the sentences 1–10 below you could use for the following. Write the numbers of the sentences.

A expressing a preference ....
B persuading someone to do something ....
C giving advice ....
D giving a reason ....
E explaining something ....

1 I regret that I can't help you on this occasion because ... ☐
2 I'd really rather ... than ... ☐
3 I suggest you plan what you're going to do very carefully ... ☐
4 I'm sure you'll help me ..., won't you? ☐
5 It is undoubtedly better to ... than to ... ☐
6 Provided I came to your house, your parents would take me to ..., wouldn't they? ☐
7 Let me tell you what I mean by ... ☐
8 Sorry, but I can't come because ... ☐
9 The information you require is ... ☐
10 What about going with the idea of ... ☐

2 Now decide if the sentences are formal or informal. Write F or I in the boxes.

3 Match the two halves of the sentences and put the verbs in the correct form.

1 You can usually persuade people to help you
2 Our teacher recommended checking our essays very carefully
3 I advise you to go to bed early
4 My sister recommended me
5 Why not come to my house on Friday afternoon,
6 Remember that we have to wear school uniform
7 It would be better to finish this work tomorrow
8 I suggested playing tennis yesterday,

A if your train .... (leave) early in the morning.
B when we .... (attend) the concert next Friday.
C to .... (take) up tennis rather than basketball.
D before we .... (hand) them in.
E but unfortunately it .... (be) too windy.
F rather than .... (rush) to get it done now.
G by .... (be) very polite to them.
H and we .... (work) on our science project together.

4 Complete this letter with the verbs in the correct form, using *could have*, *must have*, *should have* and *would have*.

Dear Auntie Lizzie
I realise I **(1)** ....
(write) to you earlier. You
(2) .... (think) I'd
forgotten all about you!
I just wanted to say how much I enjoyed the fantastic day out we had together. It was wonderful to see you again and spend some time together.
I don't think we **(3)** ....
(do) any more in a day if we'd tried. You
(4) .... (plan) it for
ages, thank you so much.
I particularly enjoyed the river trip we did, although I **(5)** ....
(wear) warm clothes like you did. Those small children sitting near us on the boat
(6) .... (freeze) in
their shorts!
I didn't realise we were going to have a commentary as we went down the river.
I think it **(7)** ....
(be) very boring without it. I
(8) .... (read) about the
places we were going to see before the trip, but of course I didn't, so it was great to hear all the history and amusing stories.
Thanks again,
Love Amy

Writing Part 2: Set Text

1 For each gap, change the noun in brackets into an adjective.

Some heroes and heroines are physically **(1)** .... (energy), riding horses and flying helicopters, and of course they are always **(2)** .... (bravery) in the face of danger. At such moments they are totally **(3)** .... (confidence) in themselves, and also **(4)** .... (decision), taking whatever action is necessary without hesitation. Others remain **(5)** .... (honesty) despite being faced with temptation, and **(6)** .... (patience) enough to gradually overcome many difficulties; in other words, they show great mental courage. Heroes and heroines are also willing to be **(7)** .... (responsibility) for others, and to remain **(8)** .... (loyalty) to friends and family at all times, always behaving in a **(9)** .... (care) way towards them, and being **(10)** .... (sympathy) to their problems. Of course, not many characters in books possess all these qualities!

2 Which of these phrases could be used to describe the opening of a book (O) and which the ending (E)?

1 it catches the reader's attention and holds it ....
2 it finally gives the answer to a lot of puzzling questions...
3 it sets out to tell the story of ...
4 it reveals what has been going on ...
5 it at last shows what the villain is really like ...
6 it introduces some very memorable characters
7 it begins in a way that may shock the reader ...
8 it leaves a lot of mysteries unsolved ...

3 Choose the correct words to complete this student's description of a set text.

The set text I read with my class this term is 'A Lion called Christian', which tells the **(1)** *real / true* story of a lion cub which is sold as a pet by a famous shop in London. It **(2)** *explains / refers* what happens when the **(3)** *main / chief* characters, two young Australians called Ace and John, buy him and take him to live with them in a flat in London. It's a very **(4)** *feeling / touching* story, because the three of them soon become close friends and Christian eventually **(5)** *turns / goes* into a sort of animal celebrity.

The second part of the story takes **(6)** *place / part* in Africa. Christian eventually becomes too big to be kept in a flat in London, so Ace and John teach him how to behave like a wild animal and release him into the wild.

I liked this story because it's **(7)** *actual / factual* and not **(8)** *based / relied* on imaginary events, like novels are. I was very **(9)** *attracted / motivated* to read it, and I was also able to look on the Internet for some old films about Christian, so now I know what he looked like. I'd **(10)** *suggest / recommend* you to read it if you haven't already done so.

Unit 6

Writing Part 2: Article

1 If you could visit a country you have never been to, which would you choose? Which of these things would interest you? Tick them.

the people ☐   the scenery ☐   the history ☐
the language ☐   the climate ☐   the food ☐
the lifestyle ☐

2 Read the article below quickly and complete it with phrases in the box.

> it has always sounded   moved here from Italy
> one final argument   such as those of
> the one I'd most like to visit   with a long history
> with a lovely climate   why I would choose

The country I would most like to visit

Of all the countries in the world, **(1)** ....
.... is Italy. You are probably
wondering **(2)** ....
this particular country. Let me explain.

I was born in Brazil, but my grandparents
(3) .... many years
ago. Consequently, I speak a little of the language.
To me, **(4)** .... very
beautiful. In addition, my grandparents are always
talking about their homeland. They describe a
place **(5)** .... For me,
that means warm sunny summers and cold winters,
with snow in the mountains in the north. They talk
about all the world-famous cities and monuments.
Italy is a very old country **(6)** ....
.........................., isn't it? Certainly, this is true when
you compare it with Brazil, because Italy has
lived through many different civilisations,
(7) .... the Greeks,
Etruscans and Romans. I would love to go and see
all the famous monuments for myself.

I also know that the people will be lovely, because
they will be like my grandparents! And there
is **(8)** .... in its
favour: the food! I could eat my way around the
country!

3 Which of the things from Exercise 1 does the writer talk about?

4 Read the article again, and underline examples where the writer does the following.

1 involving the reader in what is said
2 giving examples from personal experience
3 providing more factual information in an example
4 making a humorous comment

5 Question tags are often used in articles to give the impression we are talking directly to the reader, e.g. *It's a wonderful day, isn't it?* Match A and B to make questions.

	A	**B**
1	You can help me learn Italian,	wasn't he?
2	You'll come with me to Italy,	didn't we?
3	The waiter was helpful,	does she?
4	Mum's bought the plane tickets,	should you?
5	You shouldn't do that,	can't you?
6	Tim looks like his grandfather,	won't you?
7	We arrived late,	doesn't he?
8	Alice doesn't like visiting museums,	hasn't she?

It's a wonderful day, isn't it?

6 Add the question tag to these sentences.

1 We could have arrived earlier, ... ?
2 It was a fantastic concert, ... ?
3 Tom arrived at a good moment, ... ?
4 You should have asked me, ... ?
5 They're going to be late, ... ?
6 It's never too late to change your mind, ... ?
7 Let's go to France for our holiday, ... ?
8 I'm going to meet you at the cinema at 8.00,
   .... ?
9 He isn't a very nice person, ... ?
10 Remember to lock the door when you go out,
   .... ?

7 Now write your own article about the country you most want to visit. You can adapt the article above, and use some of the phrases and linking expressions. Don't forget to add one or two question tags, will you?

Unit 7

Writing Part 2: Letter and email

1 Complete the letter with the phrases in the box.

> as a result   because   even if   instead   such as
> the kind that   then   until recently

Dear Meg

You asked for some information about fashion in my country, and where I shop. Let me start by saying that for a lot of young people like me, it's fashionable to wear sports clothes, **(1)** .... are popular all over Europe, **(2)** .... T-shirts, hoodies, joggers or jeans.

There is probably more variety of clothing for girls. Flowery dresses are in this summer, worn with flat sandals or shoes in bright colours. Orange, yellow and green are fashionable this year, which is a nice change, because **(3)** .... everyone wore black, or maybe grey. I have to say it got a bit boring, **(4)** .... there was no problem putting together an outfit that matched!

Of course, **(5)** .... we are students, we don't have the money for expensive clothes, so we just look at them and then find something similar but much cheaper to buy **(6)** .... ! **(7)** .... of these shopping habits, I spend a lot of time with my friends 'window-shopping' on a Saturday, looking at all the really famous and very expensive designer brands. **(8)** .... I go to a cheaper store to get what I can afford.

I hope I've answered your questions,

Love Anneke

2 Read the letter again and answer these questions.

1 Which two things did Meg ask Anneke to tell her about?

2 There are three paragraphs in the letter. In which paragraph(s) does Anneke:
   a give a description? ....
   b make a general comment? ....
   c offer an explanation? ....

3 Which phrases below are used at the beginning of a letter or email asking for information? Which ones are used at the end?

   Beginning: ....   End: ....

1 I hope I've given you the information you need.
2 That's all I can think of to say about ...
3 You wanted me to write and tell you about ...
4 Let me know if you have any other questions.
5 You asked me for information about ...
6 You said you would like to know about ... in my country.

4 What do young people wear in your country? Complete the chart about clothes.

	For school	At home	For a family party
Girls			
Boys			

5 Complete the email with sentences A–F.

   A and some sandals or shoes.
   B we dress well.
   C around the house.
   D that I think they are.
   E to choose the right clothes and wear fashionable colours.
   F but at the same time, you must look good.

Dear Paul

You asked me to write about clothes in my country and to tell you whether both boys and girls are interested in them. I have to say **(1)** .... That's because I live in France, where the way you look is important to everyone. From a young age we all want **(2)** .... Jeans are popular for both boys and girls in my country, but they have to fit well and be the right colour! You need to be comfortable, **(3)** .... When we relax at the weekend we simply wear jeans and T-shirts, and a hoodie or jumper when we are cold. Girls and boys wear similar things **(4)** .... However, when we dress up for a special occasion, we look very different. The girls wear a brightly coloured dress **(5)** .... The boys wear a colourful shirt, and as they get older, a jacket. Everyone makes an effort, because that is part of our culture. As a result, **(6)** ....

6 Now write out the email, dividing it into three paragraphs and adding a suitable ending.

Unit 8

Writing Part 1: Essay

1 **Look at the different kinds of food below and answer the questions.**

> biscuits cake chips eggs fish fruit
> ice cream meat nuts pasta rice salad
> vegetables

1 Which four are the least healthy?
2 Which four contain protein?

2 **When you answer an essay question, try to give more than one point of view. Read the exam question and the opinions 1–6. Which opinions are *for* the idea, and which *against*? Write F or A.**

Some people say that we should all become vegetarian and give up eating meat. What do you think?

Notes
Write about:

   1. health
   2. cost
   3. .... (your own idea)

1 It's natural to eat meat; humans have always done so. ....
2 Producing meat is expensive and contributes to problems in the environment. ....

3 You need to eat meat to get enough protein. ....
4 Vegetarians are thinner and healthier than people who eat meat. ....
5 It's wrong to kill animals so we can eat them. ....
6 Young children need to eat meat to grow and be healthy. ....

3 **In an essay you need to explain your own ideas but you can also give other people's ideas. Write O (own) or P (other people) by these phrases.**

1 I feel very strongly that ....
2 Scientists/experts have shown that ....
3 It is often said that ....
4 I certainly agree that ....
5 It is my personal belief that ....
6 Recent research has revealed that ....
7 I have often thought that ....

4 **Read this answer to the exam question in Exercise 2. Complete the essay with the words and phrases in the box.**

> because but however if in fact
> in order to moreover so

Recent research has revealed that you can be perfectly healthy without eating meat. We all need protein, (1) .... we can find it in eggs and nuts and other foods like that. (2) .... , vegetarians are generally thinner and healthier than people who eat meat. Scientists have shown that producing meat is expensive, and (3) .... animals make methane gas, they pollute the environment. It is often said (4) .... that there would be nobody starving in the world (5) .... we were all vegetarian. It's a very powerful argument.

(6) .... , the people who argue against that say that eating meat is entirely natural, and something that humans have always done. They see nothing wrong in killing animals (7) .... we can eat them, and they argue that young children need to eat red meat (8) .... grow and develop.

It is my personal belief that ...

5 **Now finish the essay above by giving your personal opinion. You should write three or four sentences, and make your conclusion clear.**

Unit 1

Listening Part 3

Exam task

1 E 2 D 3 B 4 H 5 F

> **Recording script**
>
> *You will hear five short extracts in which people are talking about their best friend. For questions 1–5, choose from the list A–H what each speaker particularly likes about their friend. Use the letters only once. There are three extra letters which you do not need to use. Play the recording twice.*
>
> *You now have 30 seconds to look at Part Three.*
>
> *Speaker 1*
>
> Well, I'm really lucky because I've known my best friend since we were at primary school together. I think one of the reasons we get on so well is that we are both a bit quiet. For example, we can sit in silence on a long journey together and feel quite comfortable. <u>I think the most important thing though is that we're definitely similar in our likes and dislikes</u>. We're both into the same films, and dress in similar styles and colours. That means a lot to both of us. Oh, and we both laugh a lot too, although not at the same things!
>
> *Speaker 2*
>
> I get kind of mad quite often at the moment, and I think that's difficult for most people! My brother and I have certainly fallen out big time. So, really, Bob is special because he doesn't take any notice of my moods. He just sort of puts up with them. And best of all <u>he's always on my side</u>. He usually has no idea why I'm angry, but that's okay with him. He's nearly always happy so he's a good person to have around. We're comfortable with each other, we enjoy each other's company and we talk for hours.
>
> *Speaker 3*
>
> There aren't many people I've known as long as Sarah. We've been friends for years. We went to each other's birthday parties when we were little, and we know each other's families really well. <u>There are lots of things we can remember doing together, and that's extremely important to our friendship</u>. We're sort of like sisters in some ways, but we don't argue – which is just as well because Sarah would always win – she's a much stronger personality than me! We're actually very different, and we have very different tastes in most things. It means there's always loads to talk about.
>
> *Speaker 4*
>
> Well, Jim's been my best mate since we started at secondary school four years ago. We do a lot of sport together and have fun. We're in the same football team. We get on because <u>he knows what affects me, you know, why I react as I do to stuff</u>. He's similar to me in that way, I guess. That's what's really good about having him as a friend. We both get really cross when we don't win something – we're very competitive. We're in the same class next year – we've both chosen science subjects so it'll be good to do some studying together too.

> *Speaker 5*
>
> My friend Annie's fun to be around, always laughing and cheerful. She loves animals, and wants to be a vet. We work together in science at school and she's so much better at it than me and is really good at remembering all the formulas and stuff, but <u>she doesn't seem to mind when I mess something up</u> – a project or an experiment – and it's the same outside school too. I really appreciate that. Annie loves riding and she's persuaded me to give it a try. We're going on Saturday, and I have to say I'm a bit nervous, but I expect I'll be all right!

Grammar

1 1 in 2 in 3 every 4 at 5 in 6 on 7 – 8 in 9 all 10 at

2 1 than 2 great / good 3 as / so 4 to 5 much / far 6 less 7 as 8 more 9 the 10 less

Reading and Use of English Part 5

1 1 brother and sister 2 cakes in a shop window 3 Because his sister has just told him that she made some of the cakes in the window.

Exam task

2 1 C 2 B 3 A

Vocabulary

1 1 A produce B involve C play D make
   2 A get B increase C change D happen
   3 A total B amount C size D number
   4 A highly B hugely C deeply D particularly

2 1 hit it off 2 takes after 3 get on well with 4 fell out with 5 have / 've been going out together 6 socialise 7 have / 've got to know 8 fell for

Reading and Use of English Part 1

Exam task

1 B 2 D 3 A 4 D 5 C 6 A 7 B 8 C

Unit 2

Reading and Use of English Part 6

1 1 yes 2 yes

2 1 B 2 C 3 A 4 C

Listening Part 1

Exam task

1 B 2 C 3 C 4 A 5 C 6 C 7 A 8 B

1 Wednesday is likely to be a very wet day

2 ... there was so much variety too, you know, pop songs in with the classical stuff ...

   Yes, no way I was expecting that.

3 as soon as I said I'd like a bit of guidance on my project, she told me exactly what I needed to know

4 he did something to his ankle, didn't he? He had to come off the pitch

5 I can see now though that I'll have to put in a lot of effort if I'm going to get anywhere – even more than I thought

6 there were complaints as some cyclists rode through the villages at tremendous speed paying no attention to residents.

7 my dad just rang to say he'll pick me up at your house afterwards instead of in town

8 you're always trying out different things

Recording script

You will hear people talking in eight different situations. For questions 1–8, choose the best answer (A, B or C). Play the recording twice.

1

You hear a teacher talking to her class about a camping trip.

Well, I know you're all looking forward to the trip, but several of you have said you're worried about camping in the cold. The good news is that it looks as though we've seen the last of freezing nights and icy mornings, so relax. Apparently, Wednesday is likely to be a very wet day, so we'll do our museum visit then, but that's it, there's no chance of stormy weather where we're going, though they might get some here while we're away. So let's hope the forecast is right, and see you at eight o'clock on Monday morning!

2

You hear two friends talking about a concert.

Girl: Great concert! That first violinist was just fabulous to watch ...

Boy: I thought he would be ... I saw him on TV the other day ... he's dead cool.

Girl: Yeah, I wish I could play the violin like that. There was so much variety too, you know, pop songs in with the classical stuff.

Boy: Yes, no way I was expecting that!

Girl: Me neither. And I loved the concert hall, really modern, looked a bit like a spaceship. I thought concert halls were all dark wood and red seats.

Boy: Some of them are. Not that one though. There was an article about it in the local paper the other day. My mum showed it to me.

Girl: Right ...

3

You hear a girl talking to her brother.

Boy: Did you get to see Mrs Kirby then? Did she tell you what you'd missed in the last lesson?

Girl: Yes, and as soon as I said I'd like a bit of guidance on my project, she told me exactly what I needed to know and I wrote it all down. She offered me some notes on how to write the introduction and conclusion but I don't need them. I know what I'm doing now. She didn't even tell me off for not giving the work in yet. So I'll finish it tonight and give it to her in the morning.

Boy: She sounds really reasonable ...

Girl: Yeah, she's great, and you'll probably get her for history next year, too.

Boy: Cool.

4

You hear two friends discussing a rugby match they watched.

Boy 1: Did you see the France-Wales match on TV last night? Exciting stuff – and Wales won! No wonder all those fans rushed onto the pitch when the match had finished. Everyone was over the moon!

Boy 2: Yeah, I was too. I watched it with my dad. What happened to Gareth Jones though – did the referee decide he was in the wrong over that tackle?

Boy 1: Nah, it was OK but he did something to his ankle, didn't he? He had to come off the pitch. Don't think it's serious though ... he's in the team for next Saturday.

Boy 2: Great, I'll be watching that too ... want to come round to my place and watch it with me?

5

You hear a boy telling a girl about a lesson he has just had.

Girl: What was your first Russian lesson like, Joe?

Boy: Well, the teacher spoke only Russian for the first half an hour but we learnt to say our names and a few other things!

Girl: I didn't choose Russian as I thought it might be hard with the different alphabet.

Boy: Yeah – it isn't as easy for us as some other languages. I was going to do Spanish but I like a challenge so this is good for me. I can see now though that I'll have to put in a lot of effort if I'm going to get anywhere – even more than I thought – but I'm OK with that.

6

You hear a news report about a cycle ride.

The annual 50 kilometre cycle ride around Middleton took place today. 10,000 cyclists had registered. That's the maximum so people who turned up on the day couldn't join in unfortunately. We'd had a lot of rain and there was a worry that some of the roads might be muddy but it was all OK in the end. There's a prize for the fastest time and there were complaints as some cyclists rode through the villages at tremendous speed paying no attention to residents. That's not in the spirit of the day which is a community event for everyone to enjoy. And for the most part everyone did just that!

7

You hear a girl leaving a message on an answerphone.

Hi, Louisa. I'm on my way. I'll be there in about 20 minutes. I've just had my music lesson. I'm a bit later than I said as I stayed behind to have a chat with my teacher – she's really nice. I'm just walking to your place and then we'll catch the bus together to the cinema. We'll have to get the bus back too because my dad just rang to say he'll pick me up at your house afterwards instead of in town as he's got to work late now. I bumped into Jamie this morning who was with a few friends and he said he might come so I told him what time.

8

You hear two friends talking about surfing.

Girl:	Hi, Ben. Have you been surfing again?
Boy:	Yeah, I love it. I know you've never tried, Anna, but you should.
Girl:	Not sure – I'm not a very good swimmer.
Boy:	Good enough. You're so sporty – <u>you're always trying out different things</u>. Surfing would be another one to add to your list. You could be really good at it and I could show you what to do. And I know the best places to go – there are loads round here.
Girl:	But I'm not very competitive.
Boy:	It's not about that so much – you get to know the other people and that makes you try harder when you watch them – but it's more about your own satisfaction.

Grammar

1 **1** C

2 C

3 We used to live in the city centre, but we live in the country now.

4 C

5 C

6 John used to be able to play the guitar well, but he's forgotten everything now.

7 C

8 I didn't use to / didn't like ice cream when I was young because it was too cold.

2 **1** for **2** since **3** ago **4** for **5** ago **6** Since **7** since **8** for

Vocabulary

1 **Across: 4** relaxing **5** disappointing **9** thrilling **11** embarrassed **13** astonished **14** exhausting

Down: 1 fascinated **2** disappointed **3** fascinating **6** thrilled **7** impressed **8** astonishing **10** relaxed **12** worried

2 **1** criticism **2** championship **3** darkness **4** fitness **5** friendship **6** happiness **7** illness **8** journalism **9** laziness **10** membership **11** relationship **12** weakness

3 **1** careful / careless **2** childish / childless **3** foolish **4** harmful / harmless **5** predictable **6** priceless **7** profitable **8** selfish / selfless **9** stylish **10** usable / useful / useless

4 **1** adj – predictable **2** n – criticism **3** adj – selfish **4** n – laziness **5** n – championship **6** adj – useless **7** adj – priceless **8** adj – childish **9** n – fitness **10** n – membership

Reading and Use of English Part 3

Exam task

1 freedom **2** tourism **3** originally **4** height **5** inexperienced **6** responsibility **7** carelessness **8** frightening

Unit 3

Listening Part 4

1 **1** B **2** D **3** A **4** C

2 **1** ✓ **2** ✓ **3** ✓ **4** ✗ **5** ✗ **6** ✓ **7** ✗

Exam task

1 C **2** B **3** C **4** B **5** A **6** A **7** C

Recording script

You will hear an interview with Jasmine Chang, who is studying at circus school. For questions 1–7, choose the best answer (A, B or C). Play the recording twice.

You now have one minute to look at Part Four.

Interviewer:	And today we have Jasmine Chang in the studio, who's going to talk about circus school and working for a circus. Welcome Jasmine.
Jasmine:	Thanks.
Int:	So Jasmine, what does a day at circus school consist of?
Jasmine:	Well, in some ways it's just like regular school – (1) <u>my days are packed with classes</u>. Not only physical stuff like acrobatics, movement and ballet, but also theatre, music and circus history. We have classes from nine till four, and then there's extra time for individual training. It's really full on. You have to be keen to keep up with it all.
Int:	And what made you decide to go to circus school?
Jasmine:	Well, ever since I was a little girl I've loved everything about the circus. My family could never really understand it. At first it was the bright lights and the clothes. (2) <u>Then I realised that because I was good at gymnastics, if I studied I could become a circus star myself</u>. And what I like is that circus school challenges me – I learn something new every day.
Int:	And you've already performed in front of an audience, haven't you?
Jasmine:	Well ... I've done (3) <u>hundreds of acrobatics workshops with children</u>, and I've been to lots of events. That's included everything from helping to make clown costumes at a summer festival to giving a talk with a friend about how to be a trapeze performer! And to be honest, I've enjoyed them all.
Int:	But it must take such a lot of effort for a show to run smoothly and to get everything to a high standard.
Jasmine:	Well, if you're doing acrobatics of any kind like me, you obviously need to be very flexible. For trapeze, you need a lot of upper body strength to keep yourself swinging backwards and forwards. That's not so important for all the performers, like clowns for instance. For the audience, it should all look as though we're hardly trying – that it's effortless. But to achieve that, (4) <u>what every circus act needs is months of practice</u> so that the performers are almost doing everything automatically and smoothly even though it's often quite dangerous.

Int:	Are there any interesting jobs for people to do behind the scenes at the circus?
Jasmine:	Oh yeah, if you don't think you have what it takes to be constantly performing on stage, there are lots of jobs like designing scenery that don't require physical activity. You can also work backstage with the costumes and helping the performers with their make-up. And the big circus companies take on people with technical skills, (5) <u>working with the microphones and lights. That's the really interesting and creative work</u>, definitely something to go for if you can.
Int:	OK, and after you've trained at circus school, how do you find a job?
Jasmine:	It depends. There are circus performers that don't work for a single circus, but instead (6) <u>try to get a part in a particular show</u>, like an actor does for different movies. That's hard in some ways, as you might not always be in work, but it's a good way to get going in a career, so I think it's the best option. It's hard to get a permanent job in a circus, and I've been told you need to be able to perform at a very high standard all the time if you want to keep your job, so there's a lot of pressure.
Int:	Is circus work particularly dangerous for performers?
Jasmine:	Well, it can be if you don't warm up properly and stretch so you don't hurt yourself. But to be honest, that's the same for lots of professions isn't it, like ballet, for example? (7) <u>You take risks in all the jobs where you are on a stage</u>. But circus is such fun. And, as with any job, if you've done all the proper training you should be fine.
Int:	It's been great talking to you, Jasmine.
Jasmine:	Thank you.

Vocabulary

1 musicians **2** composer **3** guitarist **4** recording
5 rehearsal **6** traditional **7** classical **8** conductor

Reading and Use of English Part 7

1 1 J 2 E 3 I 4 D 5 G 6 B 7 F 8 L 9 A 10 C

2 1 B 2 A 3 B 4 B 5 A 6 B 7 A 8 A

Vocabulary

1 screens **2** chat **3** celebrities **4** presenter **5** comedian
6 role **7** documentary **8** channel **9** soap **10** character

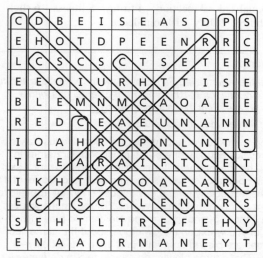

Grammar

1 1 but **2** Despite **3** in spite of **4** however **5** despite
6 although **7** In spite of **8** but

2 1 will be included **2** Is ... being filmed **3** has been done
4 wasn't given **5** was being rehearsed **6** have been made
7 was being played **8** have been given

3 1 having, cleaned **2** had, cut **3** having / going to have, painted
4 had, stolen **5** have, tested **6** had, corrected
7 have had, installed **8** had, taken

Reading and Use of English Part 4

1 had my bike fixed **2** although it had rained
3 hadn't / had not seen for **4** nobody had told me
5 is the least popular of / among **6** was frightened by

Unit 4

Reading and Use of English Part 5

1 1 suspicious **2** embarrassed **3** disappointed **4** astonished
5 discouraged **6** jealous

2 He felt disappointed.

3 D

4 B

Vocabulary

1 beat the record, energy levels, football pitch, ice rink, play rugby, score a goal, tennis court, win the cup

2 1 football pitch **2** beat the record **3** playing rugby
4 scoring a goal **5** energy levels **6** an ice rink **7** won the cup
8 tennis court

Listening Part 2

1 stick **2** goalie **3** skates **4** ice **5** puck **6** net

Exam task

1 speed **2** specialised **3** reaction **4** tiring **5** fitness **6** stick
7 helmet **8** ability **9** July **10** confidence

Recording script

You will hear a teenager called Sam Lloyd talking to his class about ice hockey. For questions 1–10, complete the sentences with a word or short phrase. Play the recording twice.

You now have 45 seconds to look at Part Two.

Well, I'm going to talk to you today about a sport I've just taken up – ice hockey. It's actually one of the most popular games in the world. You hear a lot about it, because it needs so much skill and it's a great spectator sport. It's exciting stuff, too. Some of it's really acrobatic, especially for the guy in goal! (1) <u>What appeals to me though is the speed that it's played at.</u> For me, that's what's always made it thrilling, and what made me want to play myself. So, for those of you who don't know much about the game, ice hockey matches are played on a rink, and there are six players on each team. That's three players on attack, two in defence and a goalie – that's what you call the goalkeeper – in front of the net. One of the interesting things about ice hockey is that (2) <u>goalies are really specialised players.</u> They never play in the other positions. Other players do, although they almost never play in goal.

Another thing that sets it apart from other team sports is that in ice hockey, every movement of players on the opposing team (3) <u>needs a reaction from every member of your team.</u> As there are only six players on each side, everyone has to be aware of and involved in what's going on all over the rink all the time. Now the puck – that's the rubber disc they use like a ball – goes at 90 mph, so it's busy!

You need to concentrate all the time, and that means (4) <u>it's really tiring for the players.</u> I think that's why each game consists of three periods of 20 minutes each, and the players get 15 minutes rest between them. You need time to recover!

Last season, when I started playing, I did an eight-week course for beginners at the club here in the city. It was a great way to start because (5) <u>it included basic fitness</u> and balance. Now that was really useful, as you don't want to spend your whole time falling over!

Once I'd done the basics and got the hang of the skating skills, I moved on to some special coaching sessions they did. Those were on (6) <u>stick skills</u> for ice hockey, which are very important. I thought it was good that they let you learn at your own pace, you could just ask for help and advice when you wanted it. I was dead keen, so I just kept asking!

I bought some kit of my own right away – (7) <u>the minimum you need is gloves, helmet and skates.</u> You can borrow the rest of the kit all the time you're a junior, the club has loan kit, but people buy their own protective clothing as soon as they get into a proper team. You can buy second-hand stuff, so it's not too expensive.

I've started to play in the games for juniors that the coaches organise at the club now. (8) <u>They always try and ensure the players</u> <u>are matched for ability.</u> That means they're probably the same age too. It makes the game more enjoyable and means people are less likely to injure themselves. I've been okay so far, just a few bruises!

I did my first hockey course in the summer holidays. The hockey season is basically October until April, so (9) <u>I'd say that July is a good time of year to get started</u> if you want to get involved quickly in the sport.

And I think if you do take up ice hockey, you'll really love it, and you'll learn a lot. (10) <u>I've got much more confidence now</u> than I used to have. I guess ice hockey's like other sports in that respect, you get much more from it than general fitness and learning how to play ...

So, if you're interested, go for it!

Vocabulary

1 do, make

do: your best, a course, your duty, homework, housework, research, sport

make: arrangements, changes, a decision, an effort, friends, a good impression, a mistake, a noise, a success of, a suggestion

2 **1** make, decision **2** made, good impression **3** do, homework
4 make, suggestion **5** made, mistake **6** do, duty
7 made, success **8** do, best **9** made, arrangements
10 make, effort

Grammar

1 **1** There's **2** there's going to be / will be / may be / might be
3 It's / It would be **4** Is there / Is there going to be / Will there be **5** is it **6** There hasn't been **7** Will there be / Is there
8 Will it be **9** It isn't / wasn't **10** There was / used to be

2 **1** from **2** about **3** in **4** to **5** in **6** on **7** in **8** on
9 at **10** on

3 **1** must / have to / need to remember to **2** don't need
3 haven't been able **4** can't be Peter's **5** should have phoned
6 must be **7** might have fallen **8** was able to

4 **1** might **2** can **3** should **4** must **5** shouldn't **6** can't

Reading and Use of English Part 2

1 Apart **2** order **3** instead **4** as **5** up **6** or **7** such **8** mine

Exam task

1 were **2** than **3** up **4** which **5** After **6** as **7** one **8** well

Unit 5

Listening Part 2

Exam task

1 personality 2 hairdresser 3 police 4 priorities
5 promotion 6 qualifications 7 chemist 8 money 9 chef
10 experience

Recording script

You will hear a teacher at a secondary school giving some students advice about how to choose a career. For questions 1–10, complete the sentences with a word or short phrase. Play the recording twice. You now have 45 seconds to look at Part Two.

Good morning everyone. As you know I'm here to talk to you as you start to make decisions about what careers you want to do in future. It's an exciting thing to be thinking about, and it's important to get it right. (1) You need to choose something which will match your skills, of course, but also something that you feel works for your personality as well. And the good news is that there are just so many interesting and rewarding jobs to choose from these days.

So, where do you begin? Well, it's important to choose a career that you're going to be successful in, so you need to be realistic about what you're good at. So for instance, (2) someone who likes meeting people and talking to them might enjoy being a hairdresser, but hate working as a technician, which is a job that's behind the scenes and doesn't involve much contact with people. And if you're good at handling difficult situations and (3) finding a solution after an argument, you might like to sign up with the police. You probably wouldn't be happy working for a company in an office job where there wasn't much challenge.

After that, the next step is to decide what you want from a job, so it's a good idea to sit down and make a list. (4) Write down your priorities. There are several things to consider. For example, do you want a job which gives you satisfaction and makes you feel that you've done something worthwhile at the end of the day? Alternatively, is (5) it important that you'll get promotion after a few years? These are things you really have to consider before you make any decisions.

Now, when you've reached that stage, and decided that a particular job might be for you, (6) you should find out if there are any qualifications that you need. Do you have to have a degree to do the job, or will they accept you for training without one? Knowing that might affect decisions about what you do here at school.

Moving on, another factor to consider is where the jobs you'd like to do are located. If you want to become a teacher or a nurse, there are jobs all over the country, but (7) if you want to be a chemist, you know, and work in a pharmaceutical company, there are fewer jobs, and they may not be near where you live, so you have to decide whether that will be a problem for you.

Now, there's one thing I haven't mentioned so far, and that's (8) money. I would say it's important to realise that it isn't the chief consideration when it comes to making career choices now, although it may become increasingly important as you get older. The most important things at the moment are interest and enjoyment, and finding something you have the ability to do.

And there's something else I'd like to point out. I'd definitely say that if you have a real passion for something, then see if there's a job you can do related to it. (9) So if you love cooking, why not think about becoming a chef? It may turn out to be just the job for you.

There's one final suggestion I'd like to make. Before you make any firm decisions about a long-term career, it's very important, whatever you all decide to do, (10) to try and gain some experience. Any is better than none! And if you want to be a doctor or dentist, as a few of you have already mentioned, you may find that medical schools will only consider your application if you've already spent some time working as a volunteer in your local hospital.

OK, I hope that's given you all a clear idea of where to start. Now, does anyone have any questions?

Reading and Use of English Part 7

1 Film: A cameraman's view, Hollywood greats

  History: Ancient Egypt, A century of food

  Language: Contemporary poets, Storytellers

  Science: The rainforest, Sea creatures, Inside the human body, 21st-century space travel

  Sport: Fun and fitness, Surf safari

2 No, they are about different camps.

  Yes, they did.

Exam task

1 C 2 E 3 C 4 D 5 E 6 B 7 C 8 A 9 D 10 A

Vocabulary

1 into 2 at 3 over 4 away with 5 out of 6 round to 7 to
8 up 9 across 10 for 11 by 12 ahead 13 on 14 through
15 off

Grammar

1 1 future 2 past 3 present 4 present 5 past 6 (near) future

2 1 had finished 2 had gone 3 saw 4 lived 5 didn't talk
   6 would let 7 hadn't lost 8 sat 9 were not / weren't
   10 had brought

3 1 I hadn't / had not shouted at 2 would / 'd rather you caught
   3 I (can) call Sam before 4 wouldn't / would not have had to
   5 hoped (that) I would get 6 in case it is / it's 7 unless my
   parents agree 8 we're / we are not / we aren't / don't get given

Reading and Use of English Part 1

Exam task

1 D 2 A 3 C 4 D 5 B 6 A 7 C 8 D

Unit 6

Listening Part 4

You will hear about: birds, the environment, famous buildings, history, plants, sport.

Exam task

1 C   2 B   3 A   4 C   5 C   6 B   7 C

Recording script

You'll hear an English girl called Annie talking about a trip her family made to Australia. For questions 1–7, choose the best answer (A, B or C). Play the recording twice.

You now have one minute to look at Part Four.

Well, it was definitely the best holiday my family's ever had. We flew into Sydney, and then just chilled out for a day.

Anyway, the first lunchtime, we were eating a burger in an outdoor café when four parrots landed on the next table. The waiter put some sugar out for them – like he would have done for his pets. Later that evening, some bats started flying around our heads. Everyone makes such a fuss about them here in the UK. People are scared of them. To Australians though, they're just part of the scenery, and (1) <u>I realised that they're used to having animals around. Town and country are all kind of mixed in together</u> – it's different from the UK.

Then, the next morning we headed off to the Blue Mountains. It's a national park outside Sydney, where we walked for miles through the eucalyptus trees. They smell wonderful, so I didn't mind the distances that Dad made us walk! There are sandstone cliffs too – the most famous ones are called The Three Sisters. They look wonderful at sunset. (2) <u>They're lit up at night, although I thought that it wasn't really appropriate to do that in a national park</u>. I loved the waterfalls though, they're not polluted and they look and sound fantastic. We spent three days there.

Then we drove on to Tobruk sheep station, which is a huge sheep farm open to the public. The stockmen who work there are like the Australian version of American cowboys. They get around the farms on horseback. (3) <u>We saw the sheepdogs working with the sheep – that was great fun.</u> They're so intelligent, they run round the sheep, over them even! We got to drink tea round a campfire, too. My dad talked to some of the older men about the history of sheep farming in Australia – it was a hard life.

Anyhow, we stayed at the farm overnight. I thought it would be incredibly quiet, but you could hear all sorts of animals as night fell! You can borrow a telescope to look at the sky, too. (4) <u>There are thousands of stars out in the bush. I had no idea it would be like that because I've always lived in a town</u>. We had to get up early the next day – we'd been warned about that though. Everything starts at dawn because it's so hot at midday.

The next day we headed back to Sydney, to the beach. Of course you can just picnic and do the usual stuff like swimming. We tried surfing too – there are loads of schools where you can get lessons. And I loved it. I was pretty good at standing up but when I did fall off, (5) <u>the board knocked me on the head a few times</u>. That spoilt it a bit for me, although I did manage to keep my mouth shut and avoid drinking the salt water! My brother loved surfing ... he's got good balance, he's done some skiing, and it probably helped him.

And finally, we went to see some of the famous sights in the city, like the Sydney Opera House, where there was a tour that Mum and I really enjoyed, and (6) <u>the Maritime Museum</u>, which had historic ships and stuff to look around. That <u>kept us all happy for hours</u>. Of course I took tons of photos, especially when Dad and I walked across the Harbour Bridge, because the views were just amazing.

So, that's it! I loved Australia. Do go if you get the chance. We want to go back. We might go to the Ningaloo Reef and go snorkelling but there are lots of other things to do which are just as exciting. You won't see the whole country in one trip, so it's best to focus on one area like we did. Australia's huge, and there are miles of empty desert. You can do trips there to see (7) <u>the cave art done by the first Australians ... go in winter</u>, when it's not so hot if you want to do that. Now, to finish ...

Vocabulary

1   1 B   2 A   3 A   4 B   5 B   6 A

2   1 keep up with   2 came out   3 turned out   4 comes out
5 turned out   6 keep up with

Grammar

1   1 Was the film <u>exciting enough</u> for you?

2 It's very late and we are <u>too</u> tired to eat.

3 We tried to light a candle but the wind was <u>too</u> strong.

4 The streets are dirty because <u>there isn't enough money</u> to clean them.

5 I think we would be <u>too</u> exhausted to enjoy the wonderful view if we cycled.

6 The month of May is best for holidays because the weather isn't <u>too hot</u>.

2   1 so   2 such   3 so   4 such   5 such   6 so

Reading and Use of English Part 2

Exam task

1 long   2 Although   3 so   4 where   5 a   6 one   7 out   8 be

Reading and Use of English Part 6

1   It started because Felix Finkbeiner gave a presentation at school about climate change, and became very interested in planting trees.

2   He has got young people in over 130 countries involved in the project and received support from Toyota.

Exam task

1 D   2 C   3 G   4 F   5 E   6 A

Grammar

1   bar of chocolate, breath of fresh air, can of soup, flash of lightning, item of clothing, means of transport, piece of advice, shower of rain, slice of cheese, tube of toothpaste

2   1 can of soup   2 tube of toothpaste   3 flash of lightning
4 breath of fresh air   5 slice of cheese   6 means of transport
7 item of clothing   8 shower of rain   9 bar of chocolate
10 piece of advice

Unit 7

Reading and Use of English Part 5

The girls are busking on the street.

Exam task

1 D   2 C   3 B   4 D   5 B   6 D

Vocabulary

Across: 1 head   **3** sure   **4** impression   **7** humour   **8** breath
9 fun   **10** temper   **11** ears   **12** trick

Down: 2 disappointment   **5** sick   **4** **6** nerves   **9** fool

Listening Part 3

1 **A** horse riding   **B** climbing in the tree tops   **C** quad biking

Exam task

1 H   2 A   3 B   4 G   5 E

Grammar

1 *to*-infinitive: aim, arrange, decide, deserve, manage, offer, pretend, refuse

-ing form: avoid, consider, imagine, involve, mention, practise, suggest

2 **1** refused   **2** managed   **3** deserved   **4** pretended   **5** avoid   **6** considered

3 **1** agreed, to come / go   **2** asked, I would help   **3** explained, to do / we must do   **4** enquired, left / leaves   **5** warned, to be   **6** told, was   **7** apologised, was   **8** wondered, had said

Vocabulary

1 stock, catalogues   **2** bargain, sale   **3** guarantee, goods
4 exchange, debit

Reading and Use of English Part 4

Exam task

1 was overtaken by Frank

2 Does anyone know where my

3 Luke should do

4 would ('d) have phoned

5 doesn't / won't let me

6 had such a quiet

Unit 8

Reading and Use of English Part 6

1 **1** True **2** True **3** False – between 10 and 15 minutes
4 True **5** False – 18 days, 21 hours and 40 minutes
6 False – 9.25 hours

Exam task

1 G **2** A **3** F **4** D **5** B **6** E

Vocabulary

breathing – lungs, consciousness – brain, diet – weight,
genetics – cells, hearing – ears, sight – eyes, skeleton – bones,
smell – nose, touch – skin

Grammar

1 The book **(which / that) I read** yesterday was very interesting.
2 Paul lives in the house over there **which / that** has a red front door.
3 I didn't understand everything **(that)** the teacher said in maths today.
4 I'd like to meet people **who / that** have the same interests as me.
5 The star had been replaced by another actor, **who** didn't have his talent.
6 I have been to the United States twice, **which** enabled me to improve my English.
7 There was a very high window in the room **which / that** was almost impossible to open.
8 I don't know the name of the boy **who is / who's** sitting in the front row.
9 At the zoo, I took pictures of animals **which / that** are in danger.
10 The teacher said we could leave early, **which** we all thought was a good idea.

Reading and Use of English Part 3

1 **1** attractive **2** communicative **3** creative **4** decisive
5 decorative **6** effective **7** extensive **8** impressive
9 offensive **10** productive **11** progressive **12** protective

2 **1** artistic **2** athletic **3** atomic **4** economic **5** enthusiastic
6 historic **7** pessimistic **8** realistic

3 **1** belief **2** choice **3** death **4** gift **5** knowledge
6 marriage **7** proof **8** laughter **9** sight **10** speech
11 thought **12** success **13** freedom **14** length **15** height
16 pride **17** strength **18** width

Exam task

1 visible **2** brightness **3** dramatic **4** locations **5** impressive
6 electricity **7** inconvenient **8** harmful

Listening Part 1

a) 2, 5, 7 **b)** 1 **c)** 3, 4, 6, 8

Exam task

1 A **2** B **3** C **4** C **5** B **6** A **7** A **8** B

Recording script

You will hear people talking in eight different situations. For questions 1–8, choose the best answer (A, B or C). Play the recording twice.

1

You hear two friends talking.

Girl: So, what did you think about that new crime thriller then?

Boy: Great. I liked the detective, he was really cool. The things he said were really amusing, and detectives aren't usually funny, are they?

Girl: Yeah, he made me laugh too. And I liked the descriptions I read of him, you know, his character, the way he dresses. I could imagine what he would look like ...

Boy: I hope they turn it into a TV series. It'd be good to have something like that to watch every week.

Girl: Yeah, they might just turn it into a film though, there's only one book I think.

Boy: Well, it'd make a great film, the plot's brilliant ... so many twists and turns ...

2

You hear a boy talking about a new video game.

Boy: ... yeah, I tried out the new game called *Search* yesterday and it's brilliant. There's the usual action stuff in it ... you know, chases and swinging from buildings and things, which lots of other games do just as well. But there's some very clever stuff too, like, there are all sorts of puzzles to solve before you can move on to the next level. You really have to use your brain for those. I thought they were cool and well ... a bit different really, you know, challenging. The graphics were good too, but they always are from that company. They're the ones that made *Mountain Run* ...

3

You hear a teacher talking to his students.

Man: Hi again, everyone. I'm sure you've remembered that we've got Joanna Sedley from the local paper coming to talk to us tomorrow morning, about how she became a journalist. If you think of any questions to ask while she's speaking, she'll answer them at the end. The reason I'm here now is that I need you to set the furniture up. We'll have circles of chairs, and I'd like you to help with that before you leave, please. Oh, and by the way, Joanna used to be a pupil here, back in the 1990s. I think the school might have changed a bit since then, don't you?

4

You hear a girl leaving a phone message for her mother.

Girl: Hi, Mum. It's Susie. Just thought I'd let you know what was happening. I'm going to be at college for another couple of hours. I'll be home about seven. I've missed the bus but there's no need to come and pick me up, because Jane's Mum's giving me a lift home. We're still practising for the show, and then we've got to try our costumes on, so it's all taking forever. Anyway, the costumes look great, so that's the good news. I'm starving though, so could you keep me some supper, please? Great, thanks, see you later.

5

You hear a girl telling a friend about her new art teacher.

Girl 1: Have you started your art classes yet?

Girl 2: Yeah, we've had about six now with the new teacher.

Girl 1: How's that going?

Girl 2: Good actually. She's very different from Mr Jones. He always wanted us to do things his way, you know, use the same techniques, work in a particular range of colours. Mrs Boyd is very relaxed. <u>She lets us do things our way, and then comes and helps us improve</u>. It's a good way of doing things. Then she shows us what well-known artists have done after we've done our own work ... so we can compare ideas I suppose ...

Girl 1: Great!

6

You hear a career advisor talking to a group of students.

Woman: Good morning everyone. This is the stage in your education when you have choices to make about the subjects and qualifications you do. There are certain subjects you'll all study for the next two years, such as maths, science and English. I know some of you've been thinking long and hard about other subjects and qualifications, and talking things through with your parents and teachers. And of course some of you have already chosen a career, so that will influence you. However, experience shows that <u>the best plan is to take qualifications in a good number of different subjects</u>, so you keep your career options open. Here's an example ...

7

You hear two students talking at school.

Boy: Hi, Laurie. How's it going?

Girl: <u>I like a lesson like this where you have to do things</u> rather than use books! I spent hours reading this morning. We've just started a new novel in my literature course.

Boy: Yeah, I prefer being hands-on. How did your <u>experiment</u> go?

Girl: OK. Look, <u>the stuff in the tube here is the right colour.</u>

Boy: Yeah, it looks like mine anyway. What about the school play – are you helping with it again?

Girl: I'd like to. I loved helping with the scenery last term, it was kind of well, creative.

Boy: You know there's a meeting after school tomorrow? I'm going.

Girl: Right, I'll go too then.

Boy: Cool!

8

You hear a boy starting to give a talk to his class.

Boy: Well, I'm going to do my talk on lions. I hope you'll like it. African lions are such beautiful animals, and they're very much under threat, from hunting and changes to the climate. So, what I'm going to do is this: I'll begin by showing you some pictures of them, so you can understand exactly what I see in them; then I'll tell you something about lions in general, and the lion family I watched in a safari park in Kenya. I hope you'll find it interesting. I think the way they live in big groups is fascinating, and every single lion has its own personality. That really surprised me.

Vocabulary

The ten expressions are: backup, bookmark, download, hard drive, login, password, restart, spreadsheet, update, webcam

F	H	K	P	E	Q	V	N	L	X	A	W	B	F	D
S	Y	U	G	K	U	R	T	M	Z	V	B	O	O	D
G	N	H	H	L	U	A	X	H	J	R	S	O	K	W
H	K	R	W	S	P	Z	O	I	A	E	L	K	Y	U
S	P	R	E	A	D	S	H	E	E	T	W	M	T	P
C	A	F	B	F	A	F	Y	U	D	A	F	A	E	Q
V	S	Z	C	X	T	V	A	S	F	T	G	R	S	N
J	S	I	A	C	E	Q	S	T	B	A	C	K	U	P
F	W	J	M	Y	T	O	R	B	X	X	T	I	C	R
A	O	K	M	J	S	G	R	E	S	T	A	R	T	I
E	R	H	D	L	A	L	E	M	G	B	U	O	B	S
Y	D	O	W	N	L	O	A	D	H	H	A	P	H	T
R	L	D	B	M	I	G	P	H	I	O	E	M	K	E
H	A	R	D	D	R	I	V	E	L	Z	C	D	M	A
C	N	T	P	B	K	N	G	L	N	D	V	A	A	P

Unit 1

1 1 For that reason 2 For example 3 As for 4 In contrast 5 though

2 A 2, 7, 8 B 4, 6, 10 C 1, 5 D 3, 9

3 1 due to / owing to 2 In addition / Moreover / Furthermore 3 with the aim of / with a view to 4 in order to 5 As a result / Therefore

4 1 owing to 2 in order to 3 with a view to 4 as a result 5 with the aim of 6 Furthermore, 7 therefore 8 with a view to 9 In addition 10 Due to

Unit 2

1 1 & 2 John is probably on a beach somewhere, and the boat is coming to rescue him. He's possibly on a desert island. Perhaps his boat had sunk because he'd been attacked by pirates or a shark. Or perhaps he'd fallen asleep and then fallen overboard.

2 Student's own story

3 The correct order is: 1 E 2 B 3 A 4 D 5 C

4 A had, sank, was B had gone / went, was / had been taking, hit / had hit C (had) had to, had passed, had changed, was coming D realised, was, found, learned / learnt E had been, had almost given up.

5 It's all right to give a story an open ending like this in the exam. A, B, D and E are all possible answers, i.e. you can think of a story that would fit. C is extremely unlikely. Pirates wouldn't come and rescue someone! (Or would they? What would be their motive?) D is less likely than the others as the race is likely to have been over for some time.

6 1 until 2 after 3 ago 4 during 5 since 6 before 7 for 8 When

Unit 3

1 1 E 2 F 3 C 4 D 5 A 6 B

2 1 H 2 G 3 E 4 C 5 A 6 D 7 B 8 F

I'd say that 'The Hound of the Baskervilles' is a book you really must read. The story takes place in a lonely and deserted place and the descriptions of it make you feel as if you are really there. I found the book quite frightening in places and as a result of that I decided never to read it late at night! Yet you are entertained because the writer builds up the atmosphere so skilfully.

At times things happen which make you think that the hound, a giant dog that is supposed to haunt the area, is supernatural. In fact it is not, and more importantly, this myth of a ghostly hound is being used as a way to frighten and kill people so that someone can inherit a large amount of money.

The famous detective Sherlock Holmes eventually finds the truth with the help of his good friend Dr Watson, and you wonder what would have happened if they had not gone to investigate.

In conclusion, I would say that in my opinion, 'The Hound of the Baskervilles' is an outstanding book. Once you start reading it, you won't be able to put it down!

3 awful N brilliant P dreadful N dull N entertaining P fantastic P fascinating P horrible N intelligent P stupid N terrible N wonderful P

4 1 brilliant 2 entertaining 3 dreadful 4 dull 5 stupid 6 wonderful

Unit 4

1 A 2, 5 B 4, 6 C 3, 10 D 1, 8 E 7, 9

2 1 F 2 I 3 F 4 I 5 F 6 F 7 I 8 I 9 F 10 I

3 1 G being 2 D handed 3 A leaves 4 C take 5 H will work 6 B attend 7 F rush / rushing 8 E was

4 1 should have written 2 must have thought 3 could have done 4 must have been planning 5 should have worn / been wearing 6 must have frozen / been freezing 7 would / could have been 8 could / should have read

Unit 5

1 1 energetic 2 brave 3 confident 4 decisive 5 honest 6 patient 7 responsible 8 loyal 9 caring 10 sympathetic

2 1 O 2 E 3 O 4 E 5 E 6 O 7 O 8 E

3 1 true 2 explains 3 main 4 touching 5 turns 6 place 7 factual 8 based 9 motivated 10 recommend

Unit 6

2 1 the one I'd most like to visit
2 why I would choose
3 moved here from Italy
4 it has always sounded
5 with a lovely climate
6 with a long history
7 such as those of
8 one final argument

3 The writer talks about: the people, history, language, climate and food.

4 The students should underline:
1 You are probably wondering ... ; Italy is a very old country, isn't it?
2 My grandparents are always talking about their homeland ... and other references to grandparents, plus writer's ideas about climate
3 ... many different civilisations such as those of the Greeks, Etruscans and Romans.
4 I could eat my way around the country!

5 1 can't you? 2 won't you? 3 wasn't he? 4 hasn't she? 5 should you? 6 doesn't he? 7 didn't we? 8 does she?

6 1 couldn't we 2 wasn't it 3 didn't he 4 shouldn't you 5 aren't they 6 is it 7 shall we 8 aren't I 9 is he 10 will you / won't you

Unit 7

1   **1** the kind that   **2** such as   **3** until recently   **4** even if
     5 because   **6** instead   **7** As a result   **8** Then

2   **1** fashion and shopping

     2 paragraphs: **a** – second paragraph   **b** – first paragraph
     c – third paragraph

3   Beginning: 3, 5, 6   End: 1, 2, 4

4   Students' own answers

5   **1** D   **2** E   **3** F   **4** C   **5** A   **6** B

6   Model answer

Dear Paul

You asked me to write about clothes in my country and to tell you whether both boys and girls are interested in them. I have to say that I think they are. That's because I live in France, where the way you look is important to everyone. From a young age we all want to choose the right clothes and wear fashionable colours.

Jeans are popular for both boys and girls in my country, but they have to fit well and be the right colour! You need to be comfortable, but at the same time, you must look good. When we relax at the weekend we simply wear jeans and T-shirts, and a hoodie or jumper when we are cold. Girls and boys wear similar things around the house.

However, when we dress up for a special occasion, we look very different. The girls wear a brightly-coloured dress, and some sandals or shoes. The boys wear a colourful shirt, and as they get older, a jacket. Everyone makes an effort, because that is part of our culture. As a result, we dress well.

I hope I've given you the information you need.

Best wishes

Toni

Unit 8

1   Suggested answers

     1 Unhealthy foods: biscuits, cakes, chips, ice cream

     2 These foods contain protein: fish, eggs, meat and nuts

2   **1** A   **2** F   **3** A   **4** F   **5** F   **6** A

3   **1** O   **2** P   **3** P   **4** O   **5** O   **6** P   **7** O

4   **1** but   **2** Moreover / In fact   **3** because   **4** in fact /
     moreover   **5** if   **6** However   **7** so   **8** in order to

5   Model answer

It is my personal belief that meat isn't good for your health if you eat large quantities. In addition, I don't think it is right that we spend millions of pounds feeding animals when people in some parts of the world have nothing to eat. I think it is unlikely that everyone will become vegetarian, but eating less meat less often would be a good start.

ACKNOWLEDGEMENTS

Author acknowledgements

The authors would like to thank their editors, Judith Greet, Ann-Marie Murphy and Diane Hall, for their expertise and constant support. Many thanks also to Matt Stephens (production project manager), Chloe Szebrat (assistant permissions clearance controller), Louise Edgeworth (freelance picture researcher), Leon Chambers (audio producer), Krysia Johnson (proof reader)

Publisher acknowledgements

The authors and publishers are grateful to the following for reviewing the material during the development process:

Susan Obiglio: Argentina; Maria Christaki: Greece; Jane Hoatson, Jessica Smith, Catherine Toomey: Italy; Katherine Bilsborough, Laura Clyde: Spain; Ludmila Kozhevnikova: Russia; Bridget Bloom, Helen Chilton, Mark Fountain, Rebecca Raynes: UK.

Thanks are also due to the teachers who contributed to initial research in to this course. In Milan, Italy: Judith Axelby, Liane Hyde, Rachel Shields, Prof. Barbagallo, Prof. Marrali; in Turin: Prof. Cook, Prof. Dickens, Prof. Grasso, Prof. Zoppas; in Genova Prof. Lovati, Prof. Risso. In Poland: teachers at Empik, Warsaw Study Centre, Warsaw University, ZS UMK. In Spain: Keith Appleby, Vicante Ferarios Maroto, Nick Tunstall, Lisa Wotton. In Switzerland: Keith Dabourn, Ms Eigner, Amy Jost, Ueli Hepp, Lori Kaithen, Eveline Reichel, Lee Walker and teachers at Berlitz, Berufschule Bulach, Sprachschule Schneiner, Liz and Michelle from the apprenticeship school.

Development of this publication has made use of the Cambridge English Corpus (CEC). The CEC is a computer database of contemporary spoken and written English, which currently stands at over one billion words. It includes British English, American English and other varieties of English. It also includes the Cambridge Learner Corpus, developed in collaboration with the University of Cambridge ESOL Examinations. Cambridge University Press has built up the CEC to provide evidence about language use that helps to produce better language teaching materials.

This product is informed by the English Vocabulary Profile, built as part of English Profile, a collaborative programme designed to enhance the learning, teaching and assessment of English worldwide. Its main funding partners are Cambridge University Press and Cambridge ESOL and its aim is to create a 'profile' for English linked to the Common European Framework of Reference for Languages (CEFR). English Profile outcomes, such as the English Vocabulary Profile, will provide detailed information about the language that learners can be expected to demonstrate at each CEFR level, offering a clear benchmark for learners' proficiency. For more information, please visit www.englishprofile.org

Text acknowledgements

The authors and publishers acknowledge the following sources of copyright material and are grateful for the permissions granted. While every effort has been made, it has not always been possible to identify the sources of all the material used, or to trace all copyright holders. If any omissions are brought to our notice, we will be happy to include the appropriate acknowledgements on reprinting.

Text on p. 19 adapted from www.choochoojohnnysfranchise.com; Telegraph Media Group Limited for the text on pp. 26–27 adapted from 'The 13 year old who has the world planting trees' by Harry de Quetteville, *The Telegraph* 29/04/2011. Copyright © Telegraph Media Group Limited 2011; Chicken House Ltd for the text on p. 28 adapted from *The Look*. Copyright © 2012 Sophie Bennett. Reproduced with permission of Chicken House Ltd on behalf of the author; Guardian News & Media Ltd for the text on pp. 32–33 adapted from 'Bring back the night, your health and wellbeing depend on it' by Russell Foster, *The Guardian* 13/07/2011. Copyright © Guardian News & Media 2011

Photo acknowledgements

T=Top, C=Centre, B=Bottom, L=Left, R=Right.

p. 4 (T): Shutterstock/© Elena Elisseeva; p. 4 (B): Photofusion/©John Powell; p. 7 (T): Thinkstock/iStock/© Michelle Malven; p. 7 (B): Getty Images/The Image Bank/© Paul Avis; p. 8: Corbis/Zero Creatives/© cultura; p. 11: Alamy/© Outdoor-Archiv; p. 13: Alamy/© Janine Wiedel Photolibrary; p. 14: Rex/© Startraks Photo; p. 19: © Bright World Images, photographersdirect.com; p. 20: Alamy/© Corbis Bridge; p. 21 (A): Shutterstock/©auremar; p. 21 (B): Thinkstock/© Stockbyte; p. 21 (C): Alamy/© Young-Wolff Photography; p. 21 (D): Getty Images/Digital Vision/© AE Pictures Inc.; p. 21 (E): Corbis/©Heide Benser; p. 23: Rolex Awards/© Marc Latzel; p. 24 (T): Thinkstock/iStock/© JoshPedder; p. 24 (BL): Shutterstock/© Debra James; p. 24 (BR): Alamy/© Aurora Photos; p. 25: Alamy/© Steve Bloom; p. 26: Getty Images/© Andreas Rentz; p. 32: Alamy/© blickwinkel; p. 34: Shutterstock/© Shukaylova Zinaida.

Illustrations by:

Richard Jones (Beehive illustrations) pp. 17, 30, 39
Kate Rochester (Pickled Ink) pp. 27, 33, 41, 43
Laszlo Veres (Beehive illustrations) pp. 5, 12, 28, 37

Design, layout and art edited by: Wild Apple Design Ltd.

Answers to Exercise 2, page 32

1 True
2 True
3 False. it lasts between 10 and 15 minutes.
4 True
5 False. It's 18 days, 21 hours and 40 minutes.
6 False. They need about 9.25 hours.